New Tastes of Texas

New Tastes of Texas

Lighter, Leaner Recipes Flavored with Tales
from the Lone Star State

by
Peg Hein

Illustrated
by
Kathryn Lewis

Published by Heinco Inc.
Austin Texas

New Tastes of Texas

By Peg Hein
Collaborator and Illustrator: Kathryn Lewis

Editor: Mary Ullrich

Cover Design by Michael Earney
Cover Illustration by Kathryn Lewis

ISBN: 0-9613881-3-7

Introduction

A lot of changes have been made in the way we cook during recent years, and this third book about Texas cooking reflects those changes. We use updated cooking equipment and methods, we take advantage of new ingredients and products, and we have developed a better understanding of how the foods we eat affect our health. Of major importance was the Surgeon General's report that by lowering the amount of fat consumed to 30% or less of calorie intake we could significantly reduce the risk of heart disease, strokes, diabetes and some types of cancer.

Our family experienced a major change in lifestyle when my husband's heart problems made it necessary to lower the amount of fat in our diet. Finding that more and more of the people we came in contact with were either on low-fat diets or wanted to be, we began trading recipes and tips on how to eat healthier without sacrificing taste. People on low-fat diets often lament having to give up certain foods they once enjoyed; and low-fat cookbooks seldom include recipes for such Texas favorites as chile, barbecue, Tex-Mex and chicken fried steak. It became a challenge for me to find ways of preparing old favorites that would reduce fat content to acceptable levels and to find new recipes for food we truly enjoyed. Our daughter Kathryn was the first to say, "You need to put these recipes in a low-fat Texas book;" and the idea was planted. To offer a diversity of cooking styles, I asked some good Texas cooks for recipes and they generously shared with me. The result is this collection of recipes to help you cook great-tasting food that is also healthy. From all of us who worked to make this book possible, we wish you good health and happy cooking.

Peg Hein

A Note from Peg

Many people are unsure just what is involved in low-fat cooking, but most are sure they won't enjoy it. I'm writing this book not as a nutritionist but as someone who considers the preparing and sharing of food one of life's great pleasures. I was once a "if it's made with butter, it's better" cook. That changed when my husband had an emergency heart bypass and we were told that a low-fat diet was necessary. I bought several low-fat cookbooks and tried out dozens of recipes. Not only were our meals low in fat, they were also low in taste. We found turkey and fish were all right but we wanted more variety and flavor. I bought two books listing the grams of fat for different foods, attended classes in low-fat cooking, learned to read the nutrition labels on food products and, through trial and error, began to develop recipes for meals we really enjoyed.

There is a great deal of information available about low-fat diets and how to figure the grams of fat allowed for your weight and level of activity. The easiest way is to determine the number of calories you consume daily, divide by three, and drop the last zero. It will probably be between 55 and 70 grams per day. It is not difficult to learn to budget your fat intake so you can enjoy foods you really like. Simple things like cooking in nonstick pans coated with vegetable cooking spray, using the right kinds of oils and margarines, trimming meats carefully and cutting the size of portions can make a big difference in the amount of fat you consume. Before long your tastes will change, the high-fat foods you once loved will no longer taste good, and you'll find them difficult to digest.

Don't consider low-fat cooking just another diet. This is the one that makes the difference. Evidence continues to mount indicating that the fat in our diet is the major factor in 30% of the health problems in America. Giving up a little fat along the way is a small price to pay for better health and weight control. Give the low-fat lifestyle a chance—you'll learn to love it.

New Tastes of Texas

Contents

NEW TASTES *of* Texas

Appetizers

Hil Country Spring

Rivera's Texas Salsa

The Riveras of San Antonio, who have Rivera's Chile Shop in El Mercado, know as much about chiles as anyone I know. Mary Lou contributed this recipe for a salsa that you can tell doesn't come from the grocery shelf. She says every variety of chile pepper has a different flavor, and she prefers to use Serrano peppers in much of her cooking. A Serrano pepper is smaller than a Jalapeño and has a slight point at the end. Use care when handling them because they can be very irritating to hands and eyes.

1 **Serrano pepper**	2 **tablespoons minced green onions**
4 **medium fresh tomatoes**	$^1/_2$ **sprig cilantro**
1 **garlic clove, chopped**	**Salt to taste**

- Place the pepper and the tomatoes on a cookie sheet and roast in a 350° oven for about 25 to 30 minutes, depending on the size of the tomatoes and pepper.
- Remove the stem from the pepper and the skin from the tomatoes. Place them in the bowl of your blender.
- Add the garlic, onions and cilantro and purée briefly. Serve with fat-free tortilla chips, baked potatoes, fish, or any dish that needs more flavor.

Makes about 2 cups
0 grams of fat per serving

Old El Paso Dip

While having dinner with some long-lost cousins, we discussed low-fat cooking and this recipe was the result. Margie Kelley of El Paso says this is a modified version of a recipe that has been a family favorite since her father Sam founded the original Old El Paso Company. It is a great dip for vegetables and chips and a tasty filling for Tortilla Roll-ups.

1   8-ounce package Neufchatel
    low-fat cheese, softened
1   cup Old El Paso MediumTaco Sauce
2   garlic cloves, minced

4   small green onions, minced
2   tablespoons chopped
    green chilies (optional)
Seasoning Salt

- Mix the cheese, taco sauce, minced garlic and onions in a medium-sized bowl; beat until well blended.
- Taste; add the green chilies if needed. (I was able to find only the Mild Taco Sauce and added the chilies for more zip.) Add Seasoning Salt to taste.

Makes about 1 cup   6 grams of fat per 2 tablespoons

Gillett Tortilla Roll-Ups

The food in El Paso is strongly influenced by the cooking of old Mexico and New Mexico, and El Pasoans have little taste for the popular Tex-Mex that is served in other cities in Texas. El Paso, the fifth largest city in Texas, is so far from other major Texas cities that it has developed its own distinct culture; its food is just one example.

8 fresh flour tortillas   1 cup Old El Paso Dip

- Spread 2 tablespoons of the dip over one side of each tortilla. Roll the tortillas fairly tight and place seam-side down in a covered dish. Freeze for 2 to 3 hours.
- While the rolls are still frozen, trim the ends and cut into 6 slices. Allow to thaw before serving. Garnish with a little chopped chives or cilantro if desired.

Makes 48 roll-ups   1 gram of fat per roll-up

Appetizers

The Alamo, the little mission that became etched in our hearts and minds as the symbol of Texas' struggle for independence, was defended almost entirely by men who were not Texas-born. They came to Texas for different reasons, from Kentucky, Ohio, Tennessee, Missouri, France, Scotland, England, and other countries and states to fight hard and die bravely. Their sacrifices became the rallying cry of the Battle of San Jacinto and strengthened the resolve of Sam Houston's army in its defeat of Santa Anna. Their dying at the Alamo forever enhanced the mystique of Texas.

Black Bean Dip

Black beans make a wonderful dip because they have almost no fat or cholesterol. Serve these with Pita Crisps or Skinny Dippers or with chips that are baked, not fried.

1 16-ounce can black beans	$^1/_4$ teaspoon Tabasco Sauce
2 garlic cloves, minced	$^1/_4$ teaspoon celery seed
2 green onions, minced	Salt to taste
2 tablespoons fresh lime juice	

- Drain the beans, reserving juice. Combine all the ingredients except the salt with $^1/_4$ cup of reserved bean juice and place in a food processor or blender.
- Process briefly, adding more juice if mixture seems thicker than desired. Continue to process until nearly smooth.
- Add salt to taste. Refrigerate for several hours before serving.

Makes 2 cups   0 grams of fat per serving

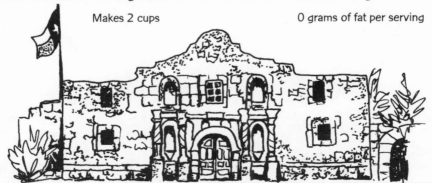

Appetizers

If I were playing the game "What historical figure would you like to invite for dinner?" I think Sam Houston would be my first choice. This complicated giant of a man's personality and idiosyncrasies are legendary. He was both loved and hated in the thirty years he dominated Texas history, and his strong and unpopular stand opposing the secession of Texas from the Union ended his political career. Beset by constant problems and controversies during his years in power, he seems very human with all his frustration and foibles. It's impossible to imagine the history of early Texas without the boldness and vision he brought to its formative years.

Judy Cecil's Chili-Olive Dip

You need to be part detective to find where a recipe originated. They often come, as this one did, from a friend who got it from a friend who got it from a friend. I managed to track it to Linda Taylor in Houston, and she told me it originally came from a fabulous cook and dear friend who had since died, and Linda wanted the recipe to bear her name.

2 $4^1/2$-ounce cans chopped green chilies	4 green onions including stems, chopped
2 $4^1/4$-ounce cans ripe olives, chopped	2 tablespoons wine vinegar
3 medium tomatoes, chopped	1 tablespoon salad oil
	Salt and pepper to taste

- Combine all the ingredients in a medium-sized bowl. Refrigerate for several hours for flavors to combine.
- Serve with tortilla chips or Doritos.

Makes 3 cups   2 grams of fat per serving

Texas Antipasto

This appetizer is good any time of the year, but it has a special appeal during the holidays. It is a tasty, low-fat, low-calorie spread that is a wonderful antidote to all the rich and fattening foods that go with the season. Serve with crackers or pita crisps.

Vegetable cooking spray
1/4 cup olive oil
1   medium cauliflower, chopped
1/2 large green pepper, chopped
1/2 large red pepper, chopped
1/2 cup sliced ripe olives
1/2 cup sliced green olives

1   cup chopped mushrooms
1   cup salsa
1 1/2 cups chunk tuna packed in
    spring water
2   4 1/2-ounce cans peeled
    tiny shrimp
1   cup low-fat Italian salad dressing

- Coat a large saucepan with vegetable spray, add the oil and place over medium heat. Add the cauliflower, green pepper and red pepper. Cook for 10 minutes, stirring frequently.
- Add the olives, mushrooms, and salsa. Simmer for 5 minutes.
- Drain the tuna and shrimp in a large colander and rinse with boiling water. Drain well and combine with the mixture in the saucepan.
- Pour the salad dressing over the antipasto and toss gently. Divide the mixture into 4 pint containers. Freeze what you will not be using within a few days.

Makes 4 pints
1 gram of fat per 2 tablespoons

Appetizers

On the grounds of the Marine Military Academy in Harlingen stands the impressive Iwo Jima War Memorial, symbol of a grateful nation's esteem for the honored dead of the U. S. Marine Corps. It depicts the famous photograph of the raising of the United States flag by Marines upon recapture of the small island of Iwo Jima in one of the fiercest battles fought in the Pacific in early 1945. Inscribed on its base are the words of Fleet Admiral Chester Nimitz: "Uncommon Valor was a Common Virtue." This massive memorial, the original working model for the bronze statue located in Arlington National Cemetery, was given to the Marine Military Academy by sculptor Dr. Felix de Weldon as an inspiration to the young cadets of the Academy. The school, a private, nonprofit college preparatory school, is based upon the traditions and leadership traits of the U.S. Marine Corps.

Ceviche

A special lady, Leona Hand, Director of the Visitors Center at the Iwo Jima Memorial Museum, enjoys preparing this tantalizing treat using any firm white fish fresh from the waters off the Texas Gulf Coast. She says mushrooms, tomatoes and green chilies are also good additions to this basic recipe.

2   pounds firm white fish, cut in bite-sized pieces
1   cup fresh lime juice
$^1/_2$ cup chopped fresh cilantro
1   diced avocado

$^1/_2$ cup chopped onion
$^1/_2$ cup sliced celery
$^1/_4$ cup sliced ripe olives
1   cup salsa or picante sauce

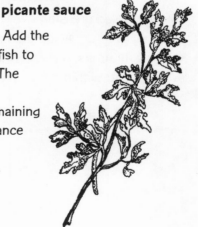

- Place the fish in a glass dish or plastic container. Add the fresh lime juice, cover and refrigerate. Allow the fish to marinate for at least 4 hours or even overnight. The marinating process, in a sense, cooks the fish.
- Drain the lime juice from the fish and add the remaining ingredients. Refrigerate so the flavors have a chance to blend.
- Serve well chilled with melba rounds or crackers.

Serves 20
$1^1/_2$ grams of fat per serving

Appetizers

The sight of a giant whooping crane dipping his beak into the water in search of a tasty blue crab is a memorable experience. A cruise on a tour boat through the marshes of the Aransas National Wildlife Refuge offers passengers this rare opportunity. Although their number has increased from fewer than 15 fifty years ago to close to 150 in recent years, these magnificent birds are teetering on the edge of extinction. They stand five feet tall and are snowy white with crimson-tipped black crowns. When you hear one give a loud, deep whoop, you'll know how it got its name.

Broiled Jumbo Shrimp

These tasty shrimp are good as an hors d'oeuvre or they can be served with rice for a great main course.

30 fresh or frozen jumbo shrimp	4 garlic cloves, minced
$^1/_2$ cup soy sauce	$^1/_2$ teaspoon black pepper
1 tablespoon oil	$^1/_2$ teaspoon freshly ground
$^1/_4$ cup lemon juice	ginger

- Thaw the shrimp if frozen. Peel, rinse, drain and pat dry with paper towels.
- Combine the remaining ingredients in a large bowl.
- Add the shrimp to the marinade, cover and refrigerate for 1 to 2 hours. Turn the shrimp occasionally.
- When ready to cook, remove the shrimp from the marinade.
- Broil about 6 inches from the broiler element for 1 to 2 minutes per side, depending on the size of the shrimp.

Serves 8

$1^1/_2$ grams of fat per serving

Crab-Stuffed Cherry Tomatoes

20 cherry tomatoes
3 tablespoons low-fat cottage
  cheese
3 tablespoons Hellmann's
  Reduced Fat Mayonnaise
1 teaspoon minced onion
1 garlic clove, minced

2 tablespoons minced celery
2 teaspoons cream-style
  prepared horseradish
$1/2$ pound crabmeat, fresh
  or canned
Chopped chives for garnish

- Cut off the top of each tomato, scoop out the pulp and turn tomato upside down to drain.
- Force the cottage cheese through a coarse sieve using the back of a large spoon.
- Combine remaining ingredients, except crabmeat and chives, with the cottage cheese in a medium-sized bowl and mix well.
- Chop the crabmeat and add to the cottage cheese mixture.
- Spoon into the tomato shells and garnish with finely chopped chives.

Serves 10   1.5 grams of fat per serving

Crab Puffs

These little appetizers taste delicious but are not filling. Make the whole batch and freeze half of them on a cookie sheet for about 2 hours. Once they are frozen, put them in a plastic bag to keep in the freezer for another time.

1   **8-ounce tub fat-free cream cheese**
2   **tablespoons fat-free salad dressing**
1   **teaspoon garlic powder**
1   **teaspoon dry mustard**

1   **6-ounce can lump crabmeat, rinsed and drained**
¹/2 cup grated Romano cheese
6   **English muffins**

- Combine the cream cheese, salad dressing and seasonings in a medium-sized bowl. Mix until smooth and creamy.
- Add the drained crabmeat and the cheese. Blend with the cream cheese mixture. Taste and add more garlic powder and cheese if you wish.
- Split the English muffins and spread the halves with the crab mixture. Cut each half into four pieces. (At this point, freeze any you want to save for use later.)
- Place the small wedges on a cookie sheet. Place the cookie sheet on a rack about 6 inches from the broiler element and broil for 6 to 8 minutes, or until puffy and golden brown.

Makes 48 pieces

¹/2 gram of fat per wedge

Mushroom-Stuffed Shells

These attractive little shells team up with the mushrooms and Mozzarella for a winning combination. The shells have no fat and can be used with any savory filling.

BREAD SHELLS:
   24 slices Pepperidge Farm very thin white bread

- Use a $2^1/_2$-inch cookie cutter to cut a circle from each bread slice. Cut a small pie-shaped wedge from circle.
- To make the bread circles more flexible, microwave them for 10 seconds on High. Press them into a miniature muffin tin to form a shell.
- Bake in a preheated 250^0 oven for 30 minutes, or until lightly browned.
- Spoon whatever filling you choose into the shells just before serving.

MUSHROOM FILLING:

Vegetable cooking spray	**$^1/_2$ pound mushrooms, minced**
1 tablespoon margarine	**$^1/_2$ cup fresh bread crumbs**
3 green onions, finely chopped	**$^1/_2$ cup grated Mozzarella cheese**
1 garlic clove, minced	**Salt and freshly ground pepper**

- Coat a large nonstick skillet with cooking spray. Heat the margarine; add the onions and garlic. Sauté for 2 minutes. Add the mushrooms; cook and stir for another 2 minutes.
- Mix in the bread crumbs, Mozzarella cheese, salt and pepper. Spoon the mushroom mixture into the Bread Shells.
- Bake in a 350^0 oven for 10 minutes.

Serves 8-10 $2^1/_2$ grams of fat each

Spinach-Stuffed Mushrooms

1 pound extra-large mushrooms
Vegetable cooking spray
1 10-ounce box frozen chopped
   spinach, thawed
3 tablespoons blue cheese fat-
   free salad dressing
1 tablespoon egg substitute

$^1/_2$ cup shredded Mozzarella cheese
$^1/_4$ teaspoon salt
$^1/_4$ teaspoon pepper
2 tablespoons bread crumbs
2 teaspoons melted margarine

- Wipe the mushrooms with a damp paper towel. Remove the stems; chop finely and set aside.
- Coat the mushroom caps with the cooking spray and place the caps, stem side up, in a glass baking dish.
- Squeeze the spinach to remove most of the water; combine with the chopped mushroom stems.
- Combine the remaining ingredients, except bread crumbs and margarine. Mix with the spinach mixture. Mound the filling into the mushroom caps.
- Mix the bread crumbs and the margarine and sprinkle lightly over top of the spinach filling.
- Bake uncovered at 325° for 25 minutes.

Serves 4   3 grams of fat per seving

Crispy Tostados

These tortilla wedges bake as light and flaky as pastry with no oil or frying. The flour tortillas are lighter but the corn tortillas have more flavor, so use the one you prefer. Crispy Tostados can be used for dips or for the Panchos below.

6 8-inch flour or corn tortillas　　Vegetable cooking spray

- Spray the tortillas on both sides with the cooking spray and cut into 6 wedges.
- Place the wedges on a large cookie sheet and spray again lightly. Bake at 400^0 for about 10 minutes, or until they are evenly browned.

Makes 36 tostados　　　　With corn tortillas - $^1/2$ gram of fat; flour tortillas - 1 gram of fat

Panchos

Refried beans in a Mexican restaurant are usually fried in either lard or bacon grease. However, there are now no-fat refried beans that are a great addition to Mexican dinners for those watching their fat intake. It makes it possible to have this tasty little antojito without feeling guilty.

36 Crispy Tostados (see above)　$^1/4$ cup jalapeño slices
1　16-ounce can no-fat refried　　1　cup grated sharp cheddar
　beans　　　　　　　　　　　　　　cheese

- Spread the tostados with the refried beans; sprinkle each tostado with about $^1/2$ tablespoon of the grated cheese.
- Top the cheese with the jalapeño slices. Place the tostados on a flat baking sheet.
- Bake at 250^0 until the cheese melts. Serve while hot.

Makes 36　　　　　With a corn tostado - $1^1/2$ grams of fat; flour tostado - 2 grams of fat

Appetizers

The Cadillac Ranch west of Amarillo is a flamboyant statement that has become an American icon. Ten cadillacs are buried in an orderly row, noses down and tail fins jutting toward the sky. It has become a mecca for people who make the pilgrimage for various reasons. Some view it as a work of art, some feel a nostalgia for the era when Cadillacs had tail fins, Yankees see it as a symbol of Texas excess and Bruce Springsteen fans come because of his recording Cadillac Ranch. Others come because it's there and they wonder why. Stanley Marsh, who bankrolled the whole thing calls the sculpture "Stonehenge for America."

Nick's Seasoned Oyster Crackers

This converted recipe of a favorite snack cuts the fat grams by 70%. Our grandson Nick loves them; and when he visits one of the first things he does is mix up a batch. It takes several hours for the crackers to absorb the oil and flavors evenly. With luck, we can keep him out of them for 30 minutes.

1 **10-ounce package oyster crackers (6 cups)**	2 **tablespoons Hidden Valley Ranch Salad Dressing Mix**
2 **tablespoons canola oil**	1 **teaspoon dill weed**
Vegetable cooking spray	

- Place one paper sack inside another. Empty the oyster crackers into the sacks.
- Spray the oyster crackers briefly with the vegetable cooking spray. Pour the oil, salad dressing mix and dill weed over the oyster crackers.
- Close the sacks and shake gently to distribute oil and seasonings evenly.
- Let the sacks set for 12 to 24 hours, turning occasionally.

Makes 12 servings   4.7 grams of fat per $1/2$ cup serving

Asparagus Roll-Ups

12 fresh asparagus spears
12 slices white or whole wheat bread
1   cup fat-free cream cheese
2   tablespoons reduced-fat
    mayonnaise

$^1/_2$ teaspoon seasoned salt
4   tablespoons no-fat bacon-
    flavored bits
1   tablespoon melted margarine
Parmesan cheese

- Snap or cut the asparagus the size of the bread. Steam the asparagus for 3 to 7 minutes, depending upon the size of the spears. They should still be slightly crisp.
- Remove the crusts from the bread and roll with a rolling pin until flattened.
- Mix the cream cheese, mayonnaise and seasoning salt. Spread evenly over the bread. Place an asparagus spear on each slice of bread and sprinkle with 1 teaspoon bacon-flavored bits.
- Roll up the bread slices and press the edges to seal. Cut each roll of bread into three pieces. Place the roll-ups on a cookie sheet.
- Brush with melted margarine and sprinkle with the Parmesan cheese.
- Bake at 400^0 for 6 to 8 minutes, or until golden brown.

Makes 36 roll-ups $^1/_2$ gram of fat per roll-up

Skinny Dippers

Dips require some method of transportation to get the dip from the container to the mouth. Usually chips, loaded with fat, are used. These wonderful little dippers work great, are low-fat and don't interfere with the flavor of the dip.

1   package brown-and-
     serve bread sticks
$^1/_2$ teaspoon onion salt

$^1/_2$ teaspoon celery salt
$^1/_2$ teaspoon garlic powder
Vegetable cooking spray

- With a serrated bread knife, cut each breadstick lengthwise into six skinny sticks.
- Combine the seasonings.
- Spray each breadstick with the cooking spray. Sprinkle the seasonings evenly over the breadsticks.
- Broil in the oven for 3 to 4 minutes, or until golden brown. (Watch carefully; turn sticks so they toast evenly.)

Makes 36 sticks   Less than 1 gram of fat per serving

Pita Crisps

4 8-inch whole wheat pitas
Vegetable cooking spray

$^1/_4$ teaspoon garlic salt
1 tablespoon Parmesan cheese

- Split each pita in half horizontally and coat each piece on both sides with cooking spray. Stack the halves and cut into pie-shaped wedges.
- Place the wedges on a cookie sheet and sprinkle with the combined garlic salt and Parmesan cheese.
- Bake in a preheated 400^0 oven for 7 to 9 minutes, or until lightly browned.

Makes 32 pieces   Trace of fat per serving

NEW TASTES *of* Texas

Breads and
Breakfast

San Antonio Mission

Banana Nut Bread

We took a favorite recipe and replaced half the margarine with buttermilk or yogurt and used egg substitute instead of 2 eggs. This removed half the fat and changed the taste and texture of the bread very little.

$^1/_2$ **cup white sugar**	**3 ripe bananas, mashed**
$^1/_2$ **cup brown sugar**	**1 teaspoon soda**
$^1/_4$ **cup margarine**	$^1/_4$ **teaspoon baking powder**
$^1/_2$ **cup egg substitute**	**2 cups flour less 2 tablespoons**
$^1/_4$ **cup non-fat yogurt or**	$^1/_4$ **teaspoon salt**
buttermilk	$^1/_2$ **cup chopped walnuts or pecans**

- Mix the sugars, margarine and egg substitute until creamy. Add the buttermilk or yogurt and the bananas. Mix well.
- Sift the dry ingredients together and add to the banana mixture. Add the nuts and stir gently until mixed.
- Pour into a greased 9x5-inch loaf pan and bake at 350° for 1 hour, or until an inserted wooden pick comes out clean.
- Let cool before slicing.

Makes 1 large loaf
$3^1/_2$ grams of fat per slice

Paris Cornbread with Green Chilies

We met Helen Mann of Paris (Texas, that is) while on a trip to Fort Davis. The conversation turned to food and it became apparent that she was a good Texas low-fat cook. She bakes this tender, flavorful cornbread in a heated 8-inch iron skillet which gives it a wonderful crust.

1   cup yellow cornmeal
1   cup unbleached white flour
1   teaspoon baking powder
$^1/_2$ teaspoon soda
$^1/_4$ teaspoon salt
1   egg

2   tablespoons canola oil
1   cup plain non-fat yogurt
$^1/_4$ cup sugar
1   4-ounce can chopped green chilies, drained
Vegetable cooking spray

- Combine the cornmeal, flour, baking powder, soda and salt in a large mixing bowl.
- Whisk the egg in a small bowl. Add the oil and yogurt and whisk until thoroughly combined. Add the sugar and green chilies and mix well.
- Make a well in the center of the dry ingredients and pour in the egg and oil mixture. Gently combine the dry and liquid ingredients until lightly mixed. The batter will be slightly lumpy.
- Lightly coat an 8-inch iron skillet or an 8-inch-square baking pan with cooking spray and place in the oven until piping hot. Pour the batter evenly into the hot pan.
- Bake in a preheated 400° oven for 30 minutes, or until the cornbread is golden and springs back when lightly touched in the center.
- Cool the bread for 10 minutes before cutting into 2-inch squares. Refrigerate any leftover cornbread.

Makes 16 pieces   2 grams of fat per piece

The little town of Gruene, a few miles west of New Braunfels, has managed to retain the flavor of a small Texas town of a long time ago. The town was founded in the mid 1840's by Henry Gruene, who offered German settlers, mostly farmers, the chance to share-crop in the new and profitable business of growing cotton. The victorian Gruene mansion, a general store, a mercantile building, a saloon and several fachwerk-style houses make you feel part of a bygone era. The Guadalupe River, lined with huge pecan and sycamore trees, flows through the town; and it's not hard to find a wonderful restaurant where you can sit under the trees, watch the river go by and wonder what life must have been like in such a place a hundred years ago.

Ginny's Skillet Cornbread

The best recipes are often very simple. For a good basic Texas cornbread, you can rely on this one. Virginia Hughes of Gruene said the recipe originally came from her stepfather, Harper Nixon, and that she has tried other recipes but thinks this is not only the best but the easiest.

1 cup stone-ground yellow
   cornmeal
^{1}/2 cup flour
1 teaspoon salt
1 teaspoon soda

1 teaspoon sugar
1 egg, slightly beaten
1 cup buttermilk
Vegetable cooking spray

- Combine all the dry ingredients in a medium-sized bowl. Combine the egg and buttermilk and mix with the dry ingredients.
- Heat two small iron skillets or two iron cornbread molds in the oven at 450°. When hot remove from the oven and coat with the cooking spray.
- Spoon the batter into the hot pans and bake at 450° for 10 to 12 minutes, or until a toothpick inserted in the center comes out clean.

Serves 6   1 gram of fat per serving

Half of the people living in Texas arrived within the last 30 years. Some of them wonder if they can be called "Texans" once they've purchased their first cowboy hat and boots. Here are some guidelines to help people know when they really are Texan; when they say "y'all" instead of "you guys"....when they hear "I was just fixin' to do that" and it doesn't sound funny....when jalapeños on nachos no longer make them gasp for water...when they learn the Texas Two-Step and the Cotton-Eyed Joe...and when the thought of living anywhere else makes them sad.

Plano Bran Muffins

These bran muffins are tender and rich in flavor. The recipe is from Jean Griffin, who lives in Plano. Any batter not used immediately will keep in the refrigerator for up to 4 weeks.

1 cup all-bran cereal	1 cup all-purpose flour
2 cups raisin bran cereal	$1/2$ cup wheat germ
1 cup boiling water	$2^1/2$ teaspoons soda
$1/3$ cup canola oil	$1/2$ teaspoon salt
$1/2$ cup egg substitute	$2^1/4$ cups buttermilk
$3/4$ cup sugar	1 cup raisins
$1/2$ cup brown sugar, packed	Vegetable cooking spray
1 cup whole wheat flour	

- Place the cereals in a large bowl and add the boiling water. Mix well.
- Combine the oil, egg substitute and sugars. Add to the cereal mixture and blend.
- Mix the flours, wheat germ, soda and salt; add alternately with the buttermilk. Stir in the raisins.
- Spoon the batter into muffin tins that have been coated with cooking spray. Bake in a 400° oven for 20 minutes.

Makes 36 muffins $2^1/2$ grams of fat per muffin

Salado Oatmeal Muffins

The recipe for these delectable muffins came from Wylene Williams, one of Salado's good cooks. The muffins are as special as the town they come from. Salado boasts several historical inns and homes which have been carefully preserved; and these, along with dozens of specialty stores, antique shops, and restaurants, make it a favorite place to visit. Anytime you're in Central Texas be sure to plan a stopover in one of Texas' most unique and sophisticated small towns.

1 cup regular oats	1 cup all-purpose flour
1 cup buttermilk	1 teaspoon baking powder
$^1/_2$ cup firmly packed brown sugar	$^1/_2$ teaspoon soda
$^1/_2$ cup vegetable oil	$^1/_2$ teaspoon salt
$^1/_4$ cup egg substitute	Vegetable cooking spray

- Combine oats and buttermilk in a medium bowl. Let stand for 1 hour.
- Add the brown sugar, oil and egg substitute to the oat mixture and stir well.
- In a larger bowl, combine the flour, baking powder, soda and salt.
- Make a well in the center of the dry ingredients. Pour the oat mixture into the well and stir only long enough to moisten the dry ingredients.
- Spray muffin pans with the cooking spray. Fill each cup two-thirds full.
- Bake at 400° for 20 minutes, or until lightly browned. Remove muffins from the pan immediately to prevent them from getting moist on the bottom.

Makes 12-14 muffins   9 grams of fat per muffin

To long-time Austinites, Barton Springs with its crystal-clear, constant-temperature water is hallowed ground. The Springs were named for Uncle Billy Barton, who settled there in 1837 with his two daughters, Eliza and Parthenia. When the Texas government built a fort nearby to protect the early settlers from the Tonkawa Indians, Uncle Billy wrote the government to "Come git your blasted soldiers. It's a damn sight more trouble to keep them away from my daughters than it is to fight the Indians."

Bev's Dilly Bread

This fragrant, tasty bread from Bev Dorsey is easy to make and has very little fat. It's a treat to have on hand when you're threatened with a hunger attack that might lead to snacking on chips or cookies or other high-fat goodies.

1 cake yeast	2 teaspoons dill seed
$1/4$ cup warm water	$1/4$ teaspoon soda
1 cup low-fat cottage cheese	1 teaspoon salt
2 tablespoons sugar	$1/4$ cup egg substitute
1 tablespoon onion flakes	$2^1/4$ cups flour
1 tablespoon melted margarine	

- Combine the yeast and warm water (90^0). Allow to stand for about 10 minutes.
- Combine the remaining ingredients, except flour, and add to the yeast mixture.
- Mix in the flour gradually. Turn out on a floured board. Knead until the dough is smooth. Put in a large bowl and cover with a damp cloth.
- Let rise in a warm place (about 85^0) for 50 to 60 minutes or until double in size.
- Bake for 35 to 40 minutes at 350^0. Allow to stand for 5to10 minutes after removing from the oven. Turn out onto a rack to cool.

Makes 16 slices   Less than 1 gram of fat per slice

The Texas Rangers are a big part of the mystique of Texas. Their story is one of courage and resourcefulness from the time they were the only law in the vast wide-open frontier to today, when they function as a highly specialized law enforcement body. With exhibits of photographs, weapons, memorabilia, a library and films, the Texas Ranger Museum in Waco captures the history of these men and the jobs they have been called upon to do with photographs, weapons, memorabilia, a library and films. The Rangers are our cherished heroes and their "one mob... one Ranger" and the "man who keeps on coming" reputation still fires our awe and imagination.

Waco Whole Wheat Bread

Joanie Warneke, an employee of the Texas Ranger Museum, finds that her bread machine makes it possible to have special home-baked bread with little effort. She says this recipe is for the large bread machine that makes a 1½-pound loaf.

1¹/₈	cups water	2	cups whole wheat flour
2	tablespoons margarine	2	cups bread flour
1¹/₄	tablespoons sugar	4	tablespoons non-fat dry milk
1¹/₄	teaspoons salt	2¹/₂	teaspoons dry yeast

- Combine all the ingredients in the bread pan of a large bread machine. Do not mix. Close the lid and push the Start button.

Makes 1 1¹/2-pound loaf   Less than 1 gram of fat per serving

Bread Machine White Bread

Bread machines take the guesswork out of how much to knead the dough or how long to let it rise. A friend who uses her machine frequently says this basic recipe gives her the most consistently good bread. She often substitutes ½ cup of whole-wheat flour for an equal amount of unbleached flour called for in the recipe.

³/₄ **cup ice water**	1 **teaspoon salt**
1 **tablespoon melted margarine**	2 **tablespoons sugar**
2 **cups Pillsbury's Better for**	1 **tablespoon non-fat dry milk**
Bread flour	1-1¹/₂ **teaspoons dry yeast.**

- Place the ice water and cooled melted margarine in the bread pan of the machine.
- Add the flour, salt, sugar and dry milk. Add the yeast on top of dry ingredients. Do not mix.
- Close the lid of the bread machine. Plug in the machine and push the Start button.

Makes 1 loaf   Less than 1 gram of fat per slice

Laura's French Toast with Blueberry Sauce

When our grandaughter Laura comes for a weekend, her favorite Sunday morning break-fast is French Toast with powdered sugar and lemon juice. For a special treat we some-times have Blueberry Sauce.

$^1/_2$ **cup egg substitute**	**8 slices firm bread**
$^1/_4$ **cup $^1/_2$% milk**	**Vegetable cooking spray**
1 teaspoon brown sugar	**Lemon wedges**
Pinch of ground nutmeg	**Powdered sugar**

- Combine the egg substitute, milk, brown sugar and nutmeg in a wide, flat bowl. Beat until thoroughly mixed.
- Dip the bread slices into the milk mixture. Place on a hot griddle or in a large, nonstick hot skillet which has been thoroughly coated with cooking spray. Cook until golden brown on both sides.
- Remove to the serving plates, cut the toast in half, arrange on the plates and sieve powdered sugar over the top. Add lemon wedges to squeeze over the top and serve with more powdered sugar. Or serve with the Blueberry Sauce below.

Serves 4   Less than 1 gram of fat per serving

Blueberry Sauce

2 cups frozen blueberries	**1 tablespoon fresh lemon juice**
1 tablespoon cornstarch	$^1/_3$ **cup orange juice**
3 tablespoons sugar	

- Combine the blueberries, cornstarch and sugar in a small saucepan. Stir in the lemon juice until the cornstarch is moistened.
- Add the orange juice and place over medium heat. Cook, stirring constantly, until the mixture is thickened and clear.
- Serve warm over waffles or pancakes. Refrigerate any leftovers.

Makes $2^1/2$ cups   0 grams of fat per serving

Having lost its two long-time claims to fame when its big oilfield came unbustled and its all-black college desegregated, the town of Hawkins in northeast Texas hopes to cause a flap in the tourist trade by declaring itself the Pancake Capital of Texas. Hawkins' flat-out assumption of the title is based on a native daughter, Lillian Richards, who became one of Quaker Oats' eight Aunt Jemimas promoting pancakes nationwide in 1926, a role she played for 37 years. The world's largest pancake is scheduled for flipping this fall.

Three-Grain Pancakes

These thin, tender pancakes have become one of our breakfast favorites. The corn and whole wheat flour add extra flavor as well as nutrition. The mix makes enough for 60 pancakes, so it is simple to whip up a batch using only as much as you want. What you don't use should be refrigerated until needed.

Pancake Mix:

1 cup rye flour	$^1/_3$ cup sugar
1 cup whole wheat flour	2 tablespoons baking powder
2 cups all-purpose flour	2 teaspoons salt
$^1/_2$ cup corn meal	$^1/_2$ teaspoon baking soda

- Mix the dry ingredients together. Refrigerate in an airtight jar or canister.
- When ready to make pancakes, follow the recipe below.

Makes enough for 60 pancakes   0 grams of fat

Pancakes:

$^1/_2$ cup low-fat milk	1 tablespoon vegetable oil
$^1/_4$ cup egg substitute or 1 egg	$^1/_2$ cup Pancake Mix

- Combine milk, egg substitute and oil. Add Pancake Mix to the milk mixture and blend.
- Cook on a medium-hot griddle coated with cooking spray until browned on both sides.

Makes 6 pancakes   2.2 grams of fat per pancake

Whole Wheat Crêpes with Nectarine Sauce

Tender whole wheat crêpes are wonderful with fruit fillings, and the nectarine sauce given here is a perfect accompaniment.

$^1/4$ cup egg substitute	1 tablespoon sugar
2 tablespoons margarine, melted	$^1/4$ teaspoon vanilla
1 cup skim milk	$^1/8$ teaspoon salt
$^1/2$ cup whole wheat flour	Vegetable cooking spray

- Beat the egg substitute, margarine and milk together in a medium-sized bowl.
- Add the flour, sugar, vanilla and salt; mix until smooth. (The batter may be prepared to this point and refrigerated until ready to use.)
- Coat a 7-inch crêpe pan or nonstick skillet with the cooking spray. Heat the pan over medium heat for 1 to 2 minutes, or until hot but not smoking.
- Pour in about 2 tablespoons batter, then quickly tilt and turn the pan so the bottom is coated with a thin, even layer of batter.
- Cook until the edges of the crêpe begin to brown and the crêpe can be easily loosened from the bottom of pan.
- Flip the crêpe and cook for another 20 seconds, or until done. Respray the pan before making the next crêpe.

Nectarine Sauce:

2 cups ripe nectarines, diced	2 teaspoons cornstarch
$^1/2$ cup apple juice (reserve half)	$^1/4$ teaspoon almond extract
1 tablespoon lemon juice	3 tablespoons sugar

- Combine the nectarines, $^1/4$ cup of the apple juice and the lemon juice in a medium-sized saucepan. Cook until the fruit begins to soften.
- Combine the remaining apple juice with the cornstarch and stir into the nectarine mixture. Cook for about 3 minutes, or until thickened.
- Remove from the heat. Stir in the almond extract and sugar.
- To serve, spoon the nectarine mixture evenly over half of each crêpe and fold crêpe over. Top with another spoonful of the nectarine sauce.

Makes 8 crêpes $2^1/2$ grams of fat per crêpe

NEW TASTES of Texas

Soups
and Salads

Big Bend Country

Hearty Vegetable Soup

This vegetable-packed soup is a great meatless meal. It is wonderful served with oven-toasted French bread and a tossed green salad. Make the soup the day before you plan to serve it and refrigerate it overnight. Any fat will come to the top and solidify, making it easy to remove.

2 tablespoons margarine	2 medium potatoes, diced
1 large onion, minced	6 cups beef or chicken stock
2 garlic cloves, minced	1 $14^1/2$-ounce can stewed tomatoes
4 medium carrots, diced	1 12-ounce can sweet corn
2 large celery ribs with leaves, diced	$^1/8$ teaspoon dried oregano
$^1/2$ medium head cabbage, shredded	$^1/4$ teaspoon dried basil
	Salt and pepper to taste

- Melt the margarine in a heavy 6-quart saucepan over medium heat.
- Add the onion, garlic, carrots and celery. Stir to coat the vegetables and cook for about 5 minutes.
- Add the remaining ingredients, cover and simmer over low heat for 1 hour.
- Taste to correct seasonings and serve.

Serves 8 $2^1/2$ grams of fat per serving

Lakeway Taco Soup

Most of the women in Lakeway are good cooks who would rather spend time in places other than the kitchen, so they are always on the lookout for recipes for tasty, low-fat and quick-to-prepare foods. This spicy, delicious soup fits the criteria. After browning the meat and onions, all you need to do is open cans and seasoning packets.

2 pounds extra-lean ground beef
1 large onion, chopped
1 10-ounce can Ro-Tel Diced Tomatos and Green Chilies
2 16-ounce cans stewed tomatoes
2 11-ounce cans corn, drained
1 14-ounce can golden hominy, drained

1 15-ounce can kidney beans
1 14-ounce can pinto beans
2 cups beef broth
1 2-ounce packet Hidden Ranch salad dressing mix
1 1.25-ounce packet taco seasoning mix
$^{1}/_{2}$ cup grated Cheddar cheese

- Combine the ground beef and onions in a large soup kettle. Cook over medium heat until lightly browned.
- Add the remaining ingredients, except for the cheese, and simmer for 2 to 3 hours. Add more beef broth or water if the soup becomes thicker than you like.
- Ladle the hot soup into individual bowls and sprinkle with the cheese.

Serves 12   Approximately 5 grams of fat per serving

Soups and Salads

The stars at night are big and bright at the McDonald Observatory which sits high atop Mount Locke in the Davis Mountains. This location was chosen by the University of Texas sixty years ago because of its clear air, distance from city lights which would interfere with night-viewing and relative lack of clouds in the area. At Star Parties viewers peek through a large 24-inch telescope that reveals portions of night sky in breathtaking detail. The Observatory's giant 107-inch telescope, one of the three largest in the world, is used for research by astronomers from all over the world.

Black Bean Soup

3 cups black beans
2 quarts beef broth
1 onion, chopped
3 garlic cloves, finely minced
1 medium carrot, chopped
2 teaspoons ground cumin
1/2 teaspoon oregano

1 tablespoon finely chopped
   cilantro
Salt and pepper to taste
Non-fat sour cream
Thinly sliced green onions,
   including tops

- Wash and pick over the beans. Cover with cold water to a depth of about 2 inches above the top of the beans. Soak for at least 8 hours, or overnight. Drain.
- Combine all the ingredients except the salt, sour cream and green onions in a large stock pot. Bring to a boil and skim off any foam that rises to the surface. Reduce the heat and simmer for 2 hours, or until the beans are very soft.
- Purée the bean mixture in a food processor or blender until smooth; return to the pan and reheat over medium heat.
- Ladle into individual bowls to serve. Top with a teaspoon of sour cream and sprinkle with green onions.

Serves 6-8   Less than 1 gram of fat per serving

Jalapeño-Potato Soup

*The Jalapeño-Potato Soup served at the Peach Tree Tea Room in Fredericksburg is one of our all-time favorite soups, and the recipe for it comes from **The Peach Tree Tea Room Cookbook** by Cynthia Pedregon. Her recipe, which calls for ¹/₄ cup butter or margarine, regular evaporated milk and sour cream, has been converted with her permission to this defatted version containing only a trace of fat per serving.*

1 **medium onion, chopped**	¹/₄ -¹/₂ **cup coarsely chopped pickled**
2 **tablespoons margarine**	**jalapeños and juice**
5 **pounds russet potatoes,**	4 **cups evaporated skimmed milk**
peeled and cubed	**Salt and pepper to taste**
8 **cups chicken broth**	**Low-fat sour cream and chopped**
1 **teaspoon comino (cumin)**	**green onions (garnish)**
Pinch of baking soda	

- In a large soup kettle, sauté the onion in the margarine until just tender.
- Add the potatoes, chicken broth and cumin. Cover and cook over low heat until the potatoes are tender, about 20 to 30 minutes. When done, coarsely mash the potatoes with a potato masher.
- Add the soda, jalapeños and evaporated milk.
- Stir well, adding salt and pepper as desired; simmer for another 15 minutes, stirring frequently.
- Garnish with a dollop of low-fat sour cream and chopped green onions.

Serves 16   Less than 1 gram of fat per serving

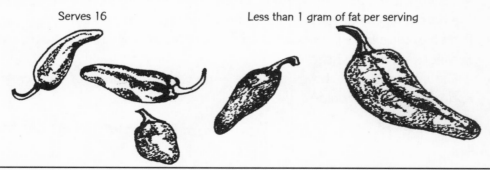

After writing five cookbooks and testing over a thousand recipes, I've reached some conclusions about recipes that I want to share with you. First, the more complicated a recipe is the worse it will taste. Second, don't mess with any recipe that lists more than two ingredients you can't pronounce. And third, don't think old recipes will be wonderful; we are much better cooks today than women were fifty years ago.

Chicken-Cheese Soup

As grocery shelves offer more and more good products that make cooking easier, cooks everywhere are taking shortcuts whenever possible. Food companies spend lots of money to get the seasonings right, so when you find a brand that you like, take advantage of their expertise. This soup tastes marvelous and is very simple to make.

2 cups cooked white chicken
1 6.6-ounce container Borden's
    Chicken Noodle Soup Starter
7 cups chicken broth

1 4.5-ounce can chopped
    green chiles
8 ounces light Velveeta cheese

- Cut the chicken into bite-sized pieces.
- Place the contents of the container of soup starter and the chicken broth in a soup kettle and simmer for 30 minutes.
- Add the chicken and green chilies and simmer for another 10 minutes. Cut the cheese into cubes, add to the soup mixture and heat until melted.
- Ladle into bowls and serve.

Serves 8   6.5 grams of fat per serving

The *cowboy was a symbol of the last frontier; and boys of all ages wanted to be like him. Hollywood made dozens of movies about this hero who could outride, out-shoot and outfight any bad guy he came across, and these movies often had the word "Texas" in their titles. Today there are Japanese and Italians and even people from New Jersey who come to Texas to see cowboys riding the range, but nowadays most Texas cowboys ride the range in their pickups. If you've ever wondered why they wear the brims of their hats turned up on the sides, it's so they can sit three abreast in a pickup. And that's the truth.*

Ranch Road Corn Chowder

1 cup onion, chopped	2 cups peeled, diced potatoes
1 cup celery, chopped	$1/2$ teaspoon white pepper
$1/2$ cup diced red pepper	Salt to taste
3 garlic cloves, minced	$1/2$ teaspoon oregano
2 teaspoons canola oil	1 12-ounce can evaporated
2 tablespoons chopped green chilies	skim milk
	1 17-ounce can cream-style corn
$1/4$ cup flour	1 12-ounce can whole-kernel
$2 1/2$ cups chicken broth	corn
$1 1/2$ cups water	Fresh parsley, chopped

- In a large saucepan over medium heat, sauté the onion, celery, red peppers and garlic in the oil until soft. Add the green chilies and mix.
- Stir in the flour and cook over medium heat until it begins to brown. Slowly add the chicken broth, stirring constantly.
- Add the water, potatoes, white pepper, salt and oregano. Cook over low heat until potatoes are tender.
- Stir in the evaporated milk and corns and bring to a boil. Ladle into soup bowls and garnish with chopped parsley.

Serves 8 $1 1/2$ grams of fat per serving

Hill Country Corn and Black Bean Salad

Black beans, yellow corn, red peppers and green onions make a great combination of colors and flavors in a salad that is better if chilled for several hours before serving.

1   16-ounce can black beans
1   16^1/2-ounce can whole-kernel corn
^{1}/2 cup chopped red bell pepper
3   green onions, chopped (including tops)
2   garlic cloves, minced

^{1}/4 cup chopped fresh cilantro
^{1}/4 cup chopped pecans
2   tablespoons salad oil
2   tablespoons soy sauce
3   tablespoons lemon juice
1   tablespoon Dijon mustard

- Drain the beans and rinse. Drain the corn and combine with the beans in a large bowl.
- Add the chopped red pepper, green onions, garlic, parsley and nuts.
- Combine the oil, soy sauce, lemon juice and mustard in a small jar with a lid. Shake well.
- Pour the dressing over the bean mixture and stir gently. Cover and marinate in the refrigerator for several hours before serving.

Serves 8
6 grams of fat per serving

Garden Tomatoes with Cucumbers

4 medium tomatoes, cut into wedges	1 tablespoon olive oil
1 cup thinly sliced cucumber	1 tablespoon water
1/2 green pepper, cut into julienne strips	1/2 teaspoon sugar
4 thinly sliced green onions	2 cloves garlic, minced
3 tablespoons white wine vinegar	1/2 tablespoon fresh basil
	1 teaspoon fresh oregano
	Salt & pepper

- Combine the tomatoes, cucumber, green pepper and green onion in a medium-sized bowl.
- Combine vinegar, oil, water, sugar, garlic, basil and oregano in a jar with a lid. Cover and shake until thoroughly mixed.
- Pour over the vegetables and toss gently.
- Refrigerate for 1 to 2 hours.
- When ready to serve, add the salt and pepper.

Serves 4   3.5 grams of fat per serfing

Fresh Dilled Cucumbers

2 tablespoons sugar	2 large cucumbers
1/4 cup water	Freshly ground black pepper
1/2 cup vinegar	Fresh chopped dill

- Place the sugar and water in a small saucepan over medium heat. Stir until sugar is dissolved. Add the vinegar and let cool.
- Peel cucumbers and cut into 1/8-inch-thick slices. Place in a medium-sized bowl.
- Pour the vinegar mixture over the cucumber slices. Add the black pepper and dill.
- Refrigerate for 3-4 hours.

Serves 6   Fat free

Frank's Place Cucumber Salad

A friend who lives in La Grange recommended this cucumber salad from Frank's Place in La Grange as "something special" so I called to get the recipe. Mrs. Denton, who prepares the salad, had to figure it out because she always makes it by taste instead of by measurement. Here's the recipe as sent to to me.

10	medium cucumbers	4	tablespoons sugar
1	teaspoon salt	1	cup vinegar
1	large onion, thinly sliced		Pepper to taste

- Slice the cucumbers, place in a large bowl and sprinkle with the salt. Let stand for 15 minutes; pour off any liquid. Add the sliced onion and mix well.
- Combine the sugar and vinegar, stirring until the sugar dissolves. Pour over the cucumbers and onions. Pepper to taste.
- Cover and refrigerate for at least one hour. Mix again before serving.

Serves 8-10   0 grams of fat per serving

Cottage Cheese & Cucumber Salad

This is a simple salad that I've made for years, but I've never seen it in another cookbook. The cottage cheese used is important, and Breakstone's gives the flavor we prefer.

2	cups low-fat cottage cheese	1	small cucumber, diced
1	tablespoon reduced-fat mayonnaise		Salt and pepper to taste
			Sliced tomatoes (optional)
3 - 4	small green onions, minced		

- Combine the cottage cheese and mayonnaise in a medium-sized bowl. Add the onions, cucumber and seasonings and stir until blended.
- Serve in a lettuce-lined bowl; or place tomato slices on a bed of shredded lettuce and top with a large spoonful of the cottage cheese salad.

Serves 4
About 3 grams of fat per $1/2$ cup serving

Bobbie's Spinach Salad

This wonderful salad with a slightly oriental flavor comes from Bobbie Lair, a good friend and a good cook. She is a person who shares my quest for that perfect recipe, one that is unusually good and has no fat, cholesterol or calories.

10 ounces fresh spinach	**1 10-ounce can mandarin**
1 5-ounce can sliced water	**oranges, drained**
chestnuts	**1 cup white grapes**

- Wash the spinach carefully, removing the stems and large veins. Pat dry and refrigerate for several hours before serving.
- When ready to serve, tear the spinach into bite-sized pieces; combine with the water chestnuts, mandarin oranges and grapes in a large bowl.

Dressing:

2 tablespoons low-sodium soy	**2 tablespoons frozen apple**
sauce	**juice concentrate**
2 tablespoons rice vinegar	**2 tablespoons olive oil**

- Combine the dressing ingredients and mix thoroughly.
- When ready to serve, add only enough dressing to lightly coat the salad ingredients. You will probably have some left to use later.

Serves 6
4^1/2 grams of fat per serving

Strawberry-Spinach Salad

This salad has an intriguing combination of flavors. You'll want to try it when the strawberries are at their best.

6	cups fresh spinach (about 8 ounces)	1 1/2	teaspoons minced fresh dill or 1/2 teaspoon dried dillweed
1	teaspoon sesame seeds	1/4	teaspoon onion powder
2	cups fresh strawberries	1/4	teaspoon garlic powder
3	tablespoons salad oil	1/4	teaspoon dry mustard
2	tablespoons red wine vinegar		A pinch of salt (optional)
1 1/2	tablespoons sugar		

- Wash the spinach carefully and remove any stems and heavy veins. Tear into bite-sized pieces. Place in a large bowl.
- Toast the sesame seeds on a cookie sheet in a 350° oven for 4 to 5 minutes, or until light brown. Sprinkle over the spinach.
- Cut any large strawberries into halves or quarters. Add the strawberries to the spinach.
- Combine the remaining ingredients in a screw-top jar. Cover and shake to mix. Chill. Shake again before using.
- Pour the dressing over the spinach mixture and toss gently.

Serves 6   7 grams of fat per serving

Layered Southwest Salad

A straight-sided glass bowl is the most effective way to show off this spectacular salad. The layers of red, yellow and green bell peppers, cucumbers, tomatoes and salad greens are colorful and the salad has a wonderful crunchy texture.

2   medium tomatoes
3   cups shredded romaine and
    iceberg lettuce
1   large sweet red pepper
1   medium sweet yellow pepper
1   medium sweet green pepper
1   cup thinly sliced celery
1   unpeeled cucumber, sliced

2   tablespoons cilantro leaves
$^1/_2$ cup shredded Mozzarella cheese
Dressing:
1   tablespoon canola oil
1   tablespoon Dijon mustard
2   tablespoons white wine vinegar
2   garlic cloves, finely minced
2   tablespoons salsa

- Chop the tomatoes into bite-sized pieces in a small bowl. Allow to stand for at least 20 minutes. Drain off any juice that accumulates in the bottom of the bowl.
- Place 1 cup of shredded lettuce in the bottom of a straight-sided glass bowl.
- Remove the stems and seeds from the peppers. Slice into $^1/_4$-inch rings. Reserve one ring from each pepper for garnish. Cut the rings in half and layer over the lettuce, arranging the outside of the rings to show through the glass.
- Add the celery and 1 cup of lettuce. Spread the tomatoes over the celery and lettuce.
- Layer the cucumbers, cilantro and the remaining lettuce over the tomatoes.
- Sprinkle the grated cheese over the top and garnish with the reserved pepper rings.
- Cover with plastic wrap; refrigerate for up to 2 hours. Combine the dressing ingredients and drizzle evenly over the top just before serving. Do not toss.

Serves 8   3 grams of fat per serving

Creamy Dilled Potato Salad

Potato salad and summer go together, and this one is good because it has enough mayonnaise to make it creamy but not so much it overwhelms the other flavors. Sometimes I mix 1/4 cup light Italian salad dressing with the mustard and mayonnaise instead of oil, lowering the fat content to less than 2 grams per serving.

4 **cups cooked unpeeled red potatoes**	3 **tablespoons vegetable oil**
2 **tablespoons chopped green onions**	2 **tablespoons white wine vinegar**
	1/4 **cup reduced fat mayonnaise**
1/4 **cup chopped celery**	1 **tablespoon prepared mustard**
1/4 **cup chopped red bell pepper**	2 **teaspoons dill weed**
	Salt and pepper to taste

- The potatoes should be cooked until they are tender but still firm. Cool and cut into 3/4-inch chunks.
- In a large bowl combine the potatoes, onions, celery and red pepper.
- Mix the oil, vinegar, mayonnaise, mustard and dill weed in a small bowl and add to the potato mixture. Mix gently.
- Add salt and freshly ground pepper to taste. Chill for 2 to 3 hours before serving.

Serves 8   6³/4 grams of fat per serving

Tangy Citrus Salad

The crunch of jicama and the tartness of the grapefruit and oranges combine with the salad greens for a great fresh tasting salad.

Vinaigrette dressing;

2 tablespoons cider vinegar	**1 teaspoon Dijon mustard**
2 tablespoons orange juice	**1 teaspoon sugar**
2 tablespoons vegetable oil	**¹/₄ teaspoon salt**

- Combine the ingredients for the dressing. Refrigerate until ready to add to the salad.

1 bunch red-leaf lettuce	**2 large oranges**
¹/₂ bunch romaine lettuce	**1 small red onion, sliced**
1 red grapefruit	**1 cup jicama sticks**

- Wash the lettuce, drain and dry by patting with paper towels. Refrigerate several hours before serving.
- Peel the grapefruit and oranges with a sharp knife to remove both the outer skin and the inner white pith. Cut out each section so it is free of any membrane.
- When ready to assemble the salad, tear the lettuce into bite-sized pieces. Combine with the fruit, onion and jicama in a large bowl.
- Pour the dressing over the greens; toss lightly to coat the lettuce mixture.

Serves 8   3¹/₂ grams of fat per serving

Asparagus Vinaigrette Salad

The bright green of the asparagus contrasts nicely with the yellow of the sieved egg yolks for a pretty and delicious summer salad. Allow 2 to 3 hours for the asparagus to marinate in the dressing before serving.

1¹/₂ **pounds small fresh asparagus**
1 **tablespoon lemon juice**
1 **tablespoon orange juice**
³/₄ **cup low-fat Italian dressing**

Shredded lettuce
2 **hard-boiled egg yolks**
Strips of red bell pepper

- Snap off the tough ends of the asparagus. Remove the scales with a vegetable peeler or small knife if desired. Arrange evenly in a vegetable steamer. Cover and steam for 5 to 6 minutes. The asparagus should be tender but still crisp.
- Rinse with cold water. Mix the lemon juice with 1 cup of ice water and pour over the asparagus to set the bright green color. Drain and place in a covered refrigerator dish.
- Combine the orange juice with the Italian dressing and pour over the asparagus spears. Cover and chill for 3 to 4 hours before serving.
- Arrange shredded lettuce on 4 chilled salad plates. Divide the asparagus evenly on the plates. Sieve the hard-boiled egg yolks over the center of the spears and garnish with thin strips of red pepper.

Serves 4
3 grams of fat per serving

Like most people, Texans have a wish list. On that list you'll find that—they wish the rest of the country would realize when they are joking and when they are being serious—they wish that people in the other 49 states would not assume that all of Texas is flat and desolate with only cacti and tumbleweeds for vegetation—they wish that visitors realized that the "Don't Mess With Texas" slogan is aimed at keeping people from throwing trash on the beaches and highways and they wish that everyone could have as much fun in life as they do.

Cranberry-Broccoli Salad

Bev Dorsey of Lakeway entertains more in a month than most people do in a year and is a fabulous cook. She and I spend hours talking about recipes, menus and what goes well together. She is responsible in one way or another for at least six of the recipes in this book and every one is choice. This recipe of hers has been approved by several tasters who agree it is a great addition to our salad section.

1	cup dried cranberries	1	small onion, finely minced
2	cups small broccoli flowerets	$^1/_2$ cup bacon bits	
4	cups shredded cabbage	$^3/_4$ cup reduced fat mayonnaise	
$^1/_2$ cup chopped walnuts		$^1/_3$ cup sugar	
1	cup raisins	2	tablespoons cider vinegar

- Combine the cranberries, broccoli, cabbage, walnuts, raisins, onion and bacon bits in a large mixing bowl.
- Mix the mayonnaise, sugar and cider vinegar and pour over the cabbage mixture. Toss well and refrigerate for several hours. This will stay crisp for up to 24 hours.

Serves 10   11 grams of fat per serving

A strong German influence is found in the names, food and customs of the area that fans out north of San Antonio. Thousands of German immigrants settled on farms and in small villages such as Boerne, Gruene, Comfort, New Braunfels and Fredericksburg. One area in San Antonio was known as Little Rhein and another neighborhood was nicknamed Sauerkraut Bend for the aroma that wafted from kitchen to kitchen on the afternoon breezes. You could spend almost every fall weekend attending wurstfests and Octoberfests and sampling the sausages, sauerkraut and baked goods prepared by good cooks in each community.

Sauerkraut Salad

4 cups sauerkraut
1 large carrot, grated
1 green bell pepper, finely chopped
1/2 cup sweet red pepper,
   finely chopped

1 cup chopped celery
1 cup chopped onion
1/2 cup sugar
3/4 cup vinegar

- Place the sauerkraut in a colander and rinse well; squeeze out most of the water. Transfer to a medium-sized bowl and add the chopped vegetables.
- Combine the sugar and vinegar and stir until the sugar is dissolved. Add to the sauerkraut mixture and toss.
- Cover and refrigerate overnight. This will keep for several days if refrigerated, and the flavor only gets better.

Serves 12
0 grams of fat per serving

East-Meets-West Cole Slaw

Kelley Jemison of Westlake Hills shares this recipe for one of the most unusual cole slaws I've ever tasted. Her original recipe called for ²/₃ cup of vegetable oil and 3 table-spoons of cider vinegar in place of the low-fat salad dressing we substituted to lower the fat content.

$1/2$ **cup sliced almonds**

2 tablespoons sesame seeds

9 cups shredded cabbage, green or red

1 bunch green onions including tops, thinly sliced

1 package Ramen oriental chicken flavored noodles, uncooked

$3/4$ **cup light oil and vinegar salad dressing**

3 tablespoons sugar

$1/2$ **teaspoon salt**

- Toast the almonds and sesame seeds in a 350⁰ oven for about 5 minutes, or until lightly browned. Watch carefully as they brown quickly.
- Toss the cabbage and green onions in a large mixing bowl.
- Remove the seasoning packet from the Ramen noodle package and set aside. Crush the noodles and add them to the cabbage mixture.
- Combine the light salad dressing, sugar and salt with the ingredients of the seasoning packet and blend well.
- Pour the dressing over the slaw mixture and toss well. Serve immediately.

Serves 10-12   4 grams of fat per serving

River Bend Fruit Medley

This combination of fruit and berries was served at a potluck picnic in the park and children and adults loved it. The tart, sweet combination of fruits is especially good with poultry. Frozen berries become mushy when thawed so cannot be substituted for canned ones.

1 16-ounce can sweet cherries	1 20-ounce can pineapple tidbits,
1 16-ounce can raspberries	(reserve $^1/_2$ cup juice)
1 16-ounce can blueberries	1 tablespoon lemon juice
1 16$^1/_2$-ounce can blackberries	Light corn syrup
1 16-ounce can pears	Sprigs of mint

- Drain the cherries and the berries. Combine in a large bowl. Chop the pears into bite-sized pieces and add to the berries.
- Drain the pineapple, reserving $^1/_2$ cup juice. Combine the pineapple juice, lemon juice and enough corn syrup to sweeten to your taste. Crush a few mint sprigs and add to the syrup.
- Pour over the top of the berries and fruit. Refrigerate for several hours before serving.

Serves 12   0 grams of fat per serving

Main Events

Blanco Town Square

Main Events

Some of Texans' favorite pastimes include wearing cowboy boots, telling Aggie jokes, going to any kind of football game, hunting anything that's legal and two-stepping around a sawdust overed floor. Another favorite activity is going over to the Coast to feast on fresh shrimp just off the boat. The accepted way to serve and partake of this treat is to cover the table with newspapers, set a big bowl of cooked shrimp and a bowl of cocktail sauce in the middle of the table and peel'em, dunk 'em and eat 'em. That's living — Texas style.

Gulf Coast Shrimp Boil

Several years ago shrimp got a bad name because of it's high cholesterol content. It is now known that saturated fat is a major factor in the production of cholesterol and that fat intake has a more adverse effect than eating foods high in cholesterol. When the nutritionists determined that shrimp, with very little fat content, could be included in a healthy diet, shrimp lovers everywhere rejoiced.

3 dozen large fresh shrimp	1 teaspoon mustard seed
3 quarts water	2 tablespoons celery seed
1/2 onion, chopped	2 tablespoons salt
2 ribs celery, chopped	1/2 lemon, sliced
1 garlic clove, minced	

- Wash the shrimp in cold water; remove the heads if you wish.
- Bring the water to boil in a large kettle. Add all the ingredients except the shrimp and the lemon. Simmer for 10 to 15 minutes.
- Add the shrimp and the lemon. Cook 3 to 5 minutes, or until the shrimp turn pink and are tender. Be careful not to overcook.
- Serve with Shrimp Cocktail Sauce (see index) and lots of napkins.

Serves 4

Less than 1 gram of fat per serving

Gardens and exhibits of wildflowers and native grasses of the United States can be enjoyed at the National Wildflower Research Center in Austin any time of the year. The Center was founded in 1982 by Lady Bird Johnson, who said she wanted to ensure that others would always be able to enjoy the wildflowers that "have enriched my life and fed my soul." The Center is committed to the study, preservation and reestablishment of native plants so that they will be part of the environment of future generations. It is a marvelous place to visit, both for the joy of learning more about our native plants and for absorbing the beauty of the gardens and meadows that are part of the Center.

Mrs. Johnson's Shrimp-Squash Casserole

Lady Bird Johnson shared this recipe for a main dish with a tasty combination of flavors. It can be prepared ahead of time if you are entertaining. If you are watching your fat intake, it is also good made with 2% milk in place of the whipping cream.

3 cups yellow squash	1 cup chicken broth
$^3/_4$ cup raw shrimp	$^1/_2$ cup whipping cream
2 tablespoons margarine	1 tablespoon finely minced onion
2 tablespoons flour	$^1/_2$ cup coarse bread crumbs
$^1/_2$ teaspoon salt	$^1/_4$ cup grated Parmesan cheese
$^1/_8$ teaspoon pepper	1 tablespoon melted margarine

- Wash and dry the squash. Cut crosswise into $^1/_4$-inch slices.
- Thoroughly rinse the shrimp under cold water and drain.
- Heat the margarine in a saucepan. Blend in the flour, salt and pepper. Cook until the mixture bubbles. Remove from the heat and add the chicken broth gradually, stirring constantly. Bring to a boil for 1 to 2 minutes.
- Blend in the cream and minced onions. Mix in the raw shrimp.
- Layer the squash in a $1^1/_2$-quart casserole dish. Spoon half of the shrimp sauce over the squash. Repeat with the remaining squash and shrimp sauce.
- Cover tightly and cook in a 400^0 oven for 30 minutes.
- Meanwhile, toss the crumbs and Parmesan cheese with the melted margarine and sprinkle over the squash and shrimp. Reduce oven heat to 350^0 and return the casserole to oven for 15 minutes, or until the crumbs are golden brown.

Serves 6   12 grams of fat per serving

Marv's Seafood Pasta

This pasta dish is my husband's specialty and he does it beautifully. It's one of our favorite recipes when entertaining a few people for a casual evening. He does most of the chopping and mincing ahead of time, but puts it together while we visit with our guests in the kitchen.

2 tablespoons olive oil	$^1/_4$ cup chopped fresh parsley
$^3/_4$ cup chopped onion	$^1/_2$ teaspoon salt
$^1/_4$ cup chopped green pepper	$^1/_2$ teaspoon black pepper
$^1/_4$ cup chopped red pepper	I pound shrimp or crab
2 large garlic cloves, minced	16 ounces angel hair pasta
2 large ripe tomatoes, peeled and chopped	Freshly grated Parmesan cheese

- Heat the oil in a large saucepan. Add the onion, peppers and garlic; sauté and stir until glossy.
- Add the tomatoes, seasonings and seafood and cook over medium heat for about 5 minutes.
- While the seafood mixture is simmering, cook the pasta according to the directions on the package.
- Drain the pasta and transfer to a large platter. Ladle the sauce over top of the pasta; sprinkle with freshly grated Parmesan cheese.

Serves 4   7 grams of fat per serving

Peppered Fish with *Creamy* Dill Sauce

This is another good way to prepare fish. The fillets are particularly good when served on a bed of cooked rice with dill sauce spooned over the top.

4 fish fillets (snapper, flounder, or catfish)

2 teaspoons olive oil, divided

2 tablespoons coarsely ground pepper

Vegetable cooking spray

- Brush the fish on both sides with 1 teaspoon olive oil; sprinkle with the pepper and gently press into the fillet. Cover and let stand for 15 minutes.
- Coat a large nonstick skillet with cooking spray.   Add the remaining teaspoon of olive oil and place over medium heat.
- Add the fillets to the pan and cook for 3 to 5 minutes on each side, or until the fish flakes easily. Remove the fish to a serving plate.
- Spoon the warm Mustard Dill Sauce over the top of the fish and serve.

Mustard Dill Sauce:

$^1/_4$ cup no-fat yogurt

$^1/_4$ cup reduced-fat mayonnaise

1 tablespoon Dijon mustard

1 teaspoon dried dill weed

- Combine all the ingredients for the Mustard Dill Sauce and mix until smooth. Heat in the microwave for 40 seconds on High.

Serves 4

About 5 grams of fat per serving

Baked Fish With Almonds

2 tablespoons sliced almonds
1 pound fish fillets (flounder,
   sole or orange roughy)
$^1/_2$ cup flour
$^1/_4$ cup Hellmann's Reduced Fat
Mayonnaise

1 tablespoon lemon juice
1 cup dry bread crumbs
1 tablespoon melted margarine
$^1/_2$ teaspoon salt
$^1/_4$ teaspoon dried dill weed

- Place the almonds in a baking dish and toast in a 350^0 oven for 5 minutes, stirring occasionally. Set aside.
- Dredge the fish fillets in the flour and place in a flat baking dish.
- Combine the mayonnaise and lemon juice; spread over the top of the fish fillets.
- Mix remaining ingredients and combine with the toasted almonds. Sprinkle over the top of the fish fillets.
- Bake, uncovered, for 12 to14 minutes at 350^0, or until fish flakes easily when pierced with a fork.
- To serve, garnish with lemon slices and parsley.

Serves 4   8 grams of fat per serving

Baked Fish Laguna Madre Style

When J. Robert Buckley moved to Brownsville, the Valley gained a really good cook. He fixes fish often and uses this simple recipe for sea trout, sole, flounder, snapper and drum. He confesses he really likes crushed potato chips sprinkled over the top of the fish instead of the stuffing; but since they are not low-fat, he doesn't usually use them.

2 6-ounce fish fillets	**1 tablespoon finely crushed**
1 tablespoon soft margarine	**Pepperidge Farm Herb Stuffing**
$^1/_2$ teaspoon dill weed	

- Rinse the fillets and pat dry with paper towels.
- Place $^1/_2$ tablespoon margarine in a 7x9-inch glass baking dish and microwave on High for 20 seconds, or until melted.
- Place the fish fillets on the melted margarine and spread with the remaining margarine. Combine the dill weed with the crushed stuffing and sprinkle evenly over the top side of the fish.
- Bake in a 400° oven for 8 minutes or until the fish flakes easily.

Serves 2   8 grams of fat per serving

Kay's Salsafied Fish Fillets

Kay Rester has another really easy and delicious way to cook almost any fish.

2 6-ounce fish fillets	**Garlic salt**
Lemon juice	**$^1/_2$ cup salsa or picante sauce**
Freshly ground black pepper	**$^1/_2$ cup shredded Mozzarella cheese**

- Rinse the fish and sprinkle with lemon juice, black pepper and garlic salt.
- Pour the salsa or picante sauce in a large skillet and place the fillets on top. Add about 2 tablespoons of water and cover. Simmer over low heat for 15 to 20 minutes.
- Remove the cover of the skillet and add the cheese. Cover and simmer a minute or two until the cheese is melted.

Serves 2   7 grams of fat per serving

Sautéed Scallops with Vegetables

Scallops are sweet and tender and have only a trace of fat. Freshness is important so ask your grocer which days scallops are delivered. Remember they cook quickly, and longer cooking will only make them tough.

1	small carrot	1	garlic clove, minced
1	small zucchini	2	cups sliced mushrooms
$^1/_2$	sweet red pepper	$^1/_4$	cup chicken broth
1	pound fresh scallops	1	teaspoon cornstarch
	Vegetable cooking spray		Salt and pepper to taste
2	teaspoons oil or margarine	2	tablespoons chopped parsley

- Cut the carrots, zucchini and red pepper into julienne strips. Set aside.
- Rinse the scallops and pat dry.
- Coat a nonstick pan with cooking spray; add the oil. Place the pan over medium-high heat. When the oil is hot, add the scallops. Cook for 4 minutes, stirring occasionally to brown the scallops evenly.
- Add the garlic and sauté for 1 minute. Take out of the pan and set aside.
- Add the vegetable strips and the mushrooms to the pan with the chicken broth.
- Place the cornstarch in a small dish. Use 1 teaspoon of the broth from the pan and mix with cornstarch until smooth. Return the cornstarch mixture to the pan. Cook and stir over medium heat until slightly thickened.
- Cook the vegetables for 4 to 5 minutes, or until just tender.
- Add the scallops to the vegetables and heat briefly.
- Season to taste. Remove to a serving dish and sprinkle with chopped parsley.

Serves 4   2 grams of fat per serving

Wedding Fajitas

*These fajitas were a rousing success when served at the wedding reception of the LeDerers' daughter in Paris, Texas. Catherine LeDerer developed the recipe especially for that occasion, and it later appeared in **Symbols of Sharing**, a cookbook celebrating the 150th anniversary of the Central Presbyterian Church of Paris. Catherine, a physician's wife, edited the church cookbook and **A Different Taste of Paris,** published by the McCuistion Regional Medical Clinic. She gives cooking lessons, helps friends plan menus to survive long family visits, and encourages her daughters in their free-lance catering.*

6 **chicken breast halves,
   skinned and boned**
Garlic salt
$^1/_3$ **cup fresh lime juice**
$^1/_3$ **cup soy sauce**
$^1/_3$ **cup Worcestershire sauce**
1 **bunch fresh cilantro**

Vegetable cooking spray
1 **cup green pepper strips**
1 **cup onion rings, cut in half**
12 **flour tortillas**
Monterey Jack cheese, grated
Salsa

- Trim chicken and flatten to an even thickness. Sprinkle generously with garlic salt.
- Combine the lime juice, soy sauce and Worcestershire sauce. Dip the chicken into the marinade mixture and place in a flat dish, layering cilantro over each piece. (Wash and drain the cilantro but do not chop.)
- Pour the remaining marinade over all, cover and refrigerate for several hours, or overnight.
- Heat a grill or nonstick skillet; spray with vegetable spray. Remove the chicken from the marinade and discard any cilantro clinging to the meat.
- Place the chicken on the grill (or in the skillet) and cook over high heat for 3 minutes on each side. Remove to a platter, slice into strips and keep warm.
- Spray the grill (or the skillet); add the green pepper and onion. Cook or sauté until translucent.
- To serve, wrap the strips of chicken, green peppers and onions in warmed tortillas. Serve with the cheese and salsa.

Serves 6-8   Approximately 9 grams of fat per serving

Chicken Flautas

Flautas are usually fried in deep fat, but these are baked until lightly browned and crispy. They are surprisingly light and flaky.

2 whole chicken breasts, cooked
Vegetable cooking spray
1 large onion, chopped
2 4.5-ounce cans chopped green chilies
1 teaspoon salt

$^1/_4$ cup light sour cream
2 cups shredded Monterey Jack cheese, divided
12 9-inch flour tortillas
Chopped lettuce
Chopped tomatoes or Pico de Gallo

- Remove the skin and bone from the chicken breasts. Using 2 forks, pull the meat apart so it is shredded.
- Coat a large nonstick skillet with cooking spray. Add the onion and cook over medium heat until softened. Add the green chilies and cook briefly.
- Remove the skillet from the heat and add the chicken, salt, sour cream and 1 cup of the grated cheese. Reserve remaining cheese for topping the flautas.
- Soften the tortillas by covering and microwaving on High for 45 seconds.
- Place about $^1/_4$ cup of the chicken mixture in a strip off-center of each tortilla; roll as tightly as possible.
- Lightly coat the tortillas with the cooking spray and bake at 375° for 15 minutes. Sprinkle the remaining cheese over the top of the flautas and bake for another 5 minutes.
- Divide the chopped lettuce between 6 serving plates. Place 2 flautas on each plate and garnish with the tomatoes or Pico de Gallo (see index).

Serves 6 $11^1/_2$ grams of fat per serving

Y'all's Texas Chicken-Spinach-Rice Ring

Sylvia and Sam Wisialowski, quintessential Texans from Houston, choose the healthy, leaner versions of Texas cooking. This rice mold of Sylvia's goes together easily, looks beautiful and tastes delicious.

3   cups chicken broth, no salt added

1 1/3 cups uncooked long-grain rice

Vegetable cooking spray

1   teaspoon margarine

2   cups sliced fresh mushrooms

1/2 cup chopped green onions

1/2 pound fresh spinach, torn into bite-sized pieces

4   4-ounce chicken breasts, cooked and shredded

1/2 teaspoon salt

1/4 teaspoon Season-All (or your favorite seasoning spice)

- Bring the chicken broth to a boil in a large saucepan. Gradually stir in the rice and simmer for 25 minutes, or until rice is tender and water is absorbed; set aside.
- Coat a large skillet with cooking spray; add the margarine and place over medium heat until melted.
- Add the sliced mushrooms and onions and sauté until tender. Add the spinach, cover and cook for 5 minutes, or until the spinach wilts. Drain well.
- Combine the rice, shredded chicken, spinach mixture, salt and Season-All in a large bowl; toss well.
- Pack into a 5-cup ring mold that has been coated with cooking spray, pressing down firmly with the back of a spoon.
- Cover with plastic wrap and let stand for 5 minutes. To keep the mold warm for a longer period of time, set it in a pan of hot water.
- Invert onto a serving platter and garnish with spinach leaves. For color, fill the center of the mold with tiny steamed carrots sliced diagonally in half.
- Y'all enjoy!

Serves 7   Approximately 4 grams of fat per serving

Spicy Chicken Stir-Fry

Dyanne Speer of Conroe says that her stir-fry varies according to what is available in the refrigerator. Sometimes she uses turkey or lean beef strips and the vegetables will vary as she uses what is on hand. And It 's fun to create a new favorite dish.

3 chicken breast halves, skinned and boned	1 cup sliced mushrooms
Vegetable cooking spray	1 cup sliced broccoli flowerets
1 large carrot, thinly sliced	1 large zucchini, washed and thinly sliced
1 medium onion, thinly sliced	2-3 tablespoons French's Bold 'n Spicy Mustard
1 bell pepper, red or green, thinly sliced	

- Cut the chicken into ¹/₂-inch strips. Coat a large nonstick skillet or wok with vegetable cooking spray and place over medium-high heat. Cook the chicken strips quickly until tender and cooked through, stirring frequently. Remove the chicken to a large plate and keep warm.
- Spray the skillet again and place over medium-high heat. Add the carrots, onion and bell pepper and cook and stir for 2 minutes.
- Add the remaining vegetables; cook and stir for another 2 minutes.
- Add the cooked chicken strips and enough Bold 'n Spicy Mustard to lightly coat the vegetables and chicken.
- Heat briefly and serve immediately.

Serves 4   2¹/₂ grams of fat per serving

Pan-Grilled Chicken Breasts

Rolling or pounding the chicken breasts to uniform thickness reduces the cooking time. This is a quick-and-easy way to prepare chicken that we really like. The fat per serving can be reduced even more by substituting low-fat Italian salad dressing for some of the oil.

4	(4-ounce) skinned and boned chicken breast halves	2	tablespoons reduced-sodium soy sauce
2	tablespoons vegetable oil	1	teaspoon grated fresh ginger
2	garlic cloves, minced		

- Place the chicken breasts between two pieces of heavy-duty plastic wrap, and flatten with a meat mallet or rolling pin to $^1/_4$-inch thickness.
- Combine the oil, soy sauce, ginger and garlic and brush over both sides of chicken breasts. Marinate for at least 30 minutes.
- Coat a large nonstick skillet with cooking spray and place over medium heat until hot.
- Add the chicken and cook on each side for 4 minutes, or until browned.

Serves 4   8 grams of fat per serving

Flat-out Garlic Chicken

When my sister Rena first gave me this recipe for microwaved chicken I had doubts about it, but it is easy to prepare and good to eat. It has become one of the recipes I use a lot. Trust the instructions for laying the chicken "flat out" and you'll have an attractive main dish. The amount of garlic in the sauce may sound like a lot, but the flavor is quite subtle.

1   **3-to-4 pound fryer**
20 large garlic cloves, unpeeled
2 tablespoons melted margarine

$^1/_2$ cup dry vermouth
Salt and pepper to taste

- Remove skin from the chicken by using a sharp knife to separate it from the meat.
- Use heavy poultry or kitchen shears to cut through both sides of the backbone and neck portion. Remove and save for soup.
- Spread the chicken, cavity side down, on a large cutting board. "Whack" the center of breast with the palm of your hand to flatten the chicken. Tuck the wings under the shoulders and turn legs so outside part is facing up.
- Place the unpeeled garlic cloves in the bottom of a large microwave-safe dish.
- Arrange the chicken, cavity side down, on top of the garlic cloves and brush with melted margarine. Add seasonings and vermouth.
- Cover the dish with plastic film wrap or wax paper, puncturing several small holes in cover for steam to escape.   Microwave on High for 22 to 25 minutes.
- Remove the chicken to a serving dish and drain the pan juices into a blender or processor. Squeeze the garlic meat into the juices and purée. (The garlic meat will pop out easily and husks can be discarded.)

Serves 4   About 10 grams of fat per serving

Houston is the biggest city in the big state of Texas and it gives the instant impression of a city of enormous energy. The world-class Texas Medical Center and the variety and scale of cultural arts offered have changed the city's image from that of a big old oil town to one of international business, research, science and culture. With unlimited shopping, Space Center Houston and the professional sports offered by the Astros, the Oilers and the Rockets, a trip to Houston offers a myriad of entertainment choices to any visitor.

Nancy Jo's Chicken Salad

A recipe from Nancy Jo Barrington is essential to any Texas cookbook I write because she has sold tens of thousands of my cookbooks over the last ten years. Now professionally involved with Jardine's Texas Foods, one of the fastest growing companies in Texas, she brings her special brand of enthusiasm to selling their products.

6   boned and skinned chicken breast halves, cooked

1   14-ounce can artichoke hearts, drained

4   ribs of celery, thinly sliced

$^1/_2$ cup green salad olives

$^1/_2$ cup Jardine's Garlic Vinaigrette Dressing, No-fat No-oil

$^1/_4$ cup Hellmann's Light Mayonnaise

Seasoned pepper to taste

Fresh fruit for garnish

- Chop the chicken breasts and artichokes into $^3/_4$-inch chunks and combine in a medium-sized bowl.
- Add the sliced celery and olives and mix.
- Combine the vinaigrette dressing with the mayonnaise and a pinch of the seasoned pepper. Add to the chicken mixture
- Toss lightly. Chill for several hours before serving. Serve with fresh fruit.

Serves 8   7 grams of fat per serving

Chicken Pasta Salad

Most women who like to cook frequently change recipes in some small way to fit their preferences. This recipe originated with Wreatha Leonard, who gave it to Nancy Elcan, who added the curry powder. When Nancy gave it to me, it called for a 10-ounce box of frozen peas, cooked briefly. When I tested the recipe, I had no frozen peas so used snow peas instead. They were so crisp and good they became my addition to the recipe.

1   12-ounce package Garden
   Spiral Pasta
1   1-ounce packet Good Seasons
   Fat-Free Italian Dressing
1   cup reduced-fat mayonnaise
1/2   teaspoon curry powder

2   cups fresh snow pea pods
1   medium onion, chopped
4   ribs celery, diced
4   cups chopped cooked
   chicken

- Cook the Garden Spiral Pasta according to package directions. Drain and cool.
- Mix the Good Seasons Italian Fat-Free Dressing following the directions on the package. Combine with the curry powder and mayonnaise. Set aside.
- Wash the snow peas, trim the ends and remove any strings. Cut into 1-inch pieces. Place in a microwave-safe dish and microwave on High for 90 seconds.
- Place the pasta in a large bowl and add the snow peas, onion, celery and cooked chicken.
- Add the dressing mixture and toss lightly. Cover and chill for at least 2 hours.

Serves 8   7.5 grams of fat per serving

Mimi's Chicken Fricassee

Chicken fricassee was a favorite Sunday dinner at our house when I was a child. Some recipes can be converted to low-fat without sacrificing taste; and this chicken tastes as good as I remember my mother's being, but it has a lot less calories and fat.

Vegetable cooking spray
6 4-ounce chicken breast
   halves, skinned and boned
2 tablespoons margarine
2 cups low-sodium chicken broth
1 cup sliced celery
1 cup chopped onion

2 . cups baby carrots
2 cups sliced fresh mushrooms
2 envelopes Lipton Cream of
Chicken Cup-a-Soup Mix
1 7.5-ounce tube ready-to-
   bake low-fat biscuits

- Coat a large nonstick skillet with cooking spray and place over medium heat. Melt the margarine in the pan. Add the chicken and cook until lightly browned.
- Remove the chicken from the skillet and place in a 3-quart casserole.
- Pour $1/2$ cup chicken broth into the skillet; simmer and stir to loosen any crusty bits of chicken in the pan. Combine the Lipton's Cup-a-Soup Mix and the remaining chicken broth in the skillet. Stir and simmer for 2 to 3 minutes, or until broth thickens.
- Combine the celery, onion, carrots and mushrooms with the mixture in the skillet. Simmer briefly.
- Spoon the vegetables and broth mixture over the chicken breast. Cover; bake at 300^0 for 30 minutes.
- Remove the casserole from the oven, uncover and place the unbaked biscuits on top of the hot fricassee.
- Increase the oven temperature to 375°. Return the casserole to the oven and bake, uncovered, for another 20 minutes, or until the biscuits are nicely browned.

Serves 6   11 grams of fat per serving

Chicken & Stuffing Casserole

If your family loves the stuffing best when you roast a chicken or turkey, you will want to try this recipe. Turkey is good when used instead of the chicken and has only 4 grams of fat per serving. It's almost like having Thanksgiving dinner and a lot less trouble. The recipe was converted to low-fat from one given me by Kay Germond.

Vegetable cooking spray
1 tablespoon margarine
$^1/_2$ cup chopped celery
$^1/_2$ cup chopped onion
2 cups chicken broth
1 10$^3/_4$-ounce can Campbell's Healthy Request Cream of Chicken Soup

1 10$^3/_4$-ounce can Campbell's Healthy Request Cream of Mushroom soup
1 8-ounce package Pepperidge Farm Herb-Seasoned Stuffing Mix
4 large skinless chicken breasts, cooked and cubed

- Coat a large skillet with cooking spray. Add the margarine, celery and onion and sauté over medium heat until tender.
- Combine the broth and soups in a large bowl. Reserve 1 cup of the soup mixture for the topping.
- Combine the stuffing mix, celery and onion with the soups.
- Layer half of the stuffing mixture in the bottom of a 9x13-inch casserole that has been coated with cooking spray.
- Spread half of the cooked chicken over top of stuffing mixture. Repeat process with remaining stuffing and chicken.
- Top with reserved soup mixture. Cover with foil and bake at 350° for 45 minutes.

Serves 8   6 grams of fat per serving

Main Events

Every spring the roadsides and hills over a large portion of Texas become a rhapsody in blue as the bluebonnets open. One of the rites of spring is to drive over favorite highways and backroads looking for the biggest, brightest patch of flowers to serve as a backdrop in photos of loved ones, babies, pets and maybe even a new car or motorcycle. The bluebonnets range in color from the palest blue to a deep royal purple. About two weeks after the bluebonnets first appear, the Indian paintbrushes open and add accent of coral here and there among the bluebonnets.

Glazed Turkey Breast

This is the easiest way I know to have beautiful slices of moist turkey breast for a special buffet. When entertaining eight or more people, be aware of the fat content in your menu because you'll probably find that at least one guest will be on a low-fat diet and two more should be. What better way to show your friends you care about them.

1 6-7 pound turkey breast
$^1/_3$ cup honey
1 tablespoon dry mustard

1 6$^1/_2$-ounce can frozen apple juice (undiluted)

- Remove the skin from the turkey breast using a sharp knife. Insert a meat thermometer into the center of the breast.
- Combine the honey, dry mustard and apple juice.
- Place the turkey breast in a medium-sized roasting pan. Baste the entire breast generously with the apple juice mixture.
- Cover the turkey breast and bake in a preheated 325° oven for 1 hour.
- Uncover and bake for another hour, or until the meat thermometer registers 180°. Baste frequently after removing the cover from the turkey.
- Remove from the oven and allow to cool for 15 to 20 minutes before slicing.

Serves 4   4 grams of fat per serving

Turkey Cutlets with Caper Sauce

These tender cuts of turkey breast prepared with a sauce of lemon juice and capers will remind you of Veal Picatta. Try it when you want something quick and easy

4 4-ounce turkey cutlets	1 garlic clove, minced
$^1/_4$ cup all-purpose flour	$^1/_2$ cup chicken broth
$^1/_2$ teaspoon salt	1 tablespoon lemon juice
$^1/_2$ teaspoon black pepper	1 tablespoon capers, drained
Vegetable cooking spray	Fresh parsley, chopped
1 tablespoon olive oil	

- Flatten the cutlets by covering with waxed paper and tapping lightly with one side of a rolling pin until cutlets are about $^1/_4$-inch thick.
- Mix the flour, salt and pepper on a plate. Dredge the cutlets lightly in the mixture. Coat a nonstick skillet with the cooking spray. Add the oil and heat. Cook the cutlets in the oil until browned, about 2 to 3 minutes on each side.
- Remove the cutlets to a warmed plate to hold.
- Add the garlic to the pan and sauté briefly. Add the chicken broth; simmer and stir to loosen any browned bits of cutlet in the pan.
- Stir in the lemon juice and capers and simmer for 1 to 2 minutes. Spoon the sauce over the cutlets, sprinkle with the parsley and serve.

Serves 4   6 grams of fat per serving

Barbecued Beef Brisket

Barbecued beef brisket is classic Texas fare and is almost always served at a "barbecue." Over half the briskets sold in the U.S. every year are sold in Texas; however, people in other states are beginning to realize how good this Texas favorite can be when cooked slowly for a long time. Buy the trimmed flat end of the brisket; then when you get it home trim the layer of fat still left on one side. Well-trimmed brisket has about 9 grams of fat in each 4-ounce serving. You probably would rather not know that barbecue joints do not trim their briskets and that one of their orders can have 40 grams of fat or more.

3	**pounds beef brisket, well trimmed**	**1**	**tablespoon liquid smoke**
1	**tablespoon Worcestershire sauce**	**1**	**teaspoon garlic salt**

- Place the brisket on a piece of heavy duty foil large enough to enclose the meat.
- Combine the Worcestershire sauce, liquid smoke and garlic salt and rub into both sides of the meat. Wrap the meat in the foil so it is tightly sealed. Refrigerate for several hours.
- Bake in a 275° oven for 4 hours. Unwrap the brisket; pour 1 cup of Barbecue Sauce over it, reseal and bake for another hour. Slice the meat against the grain and serve with the sauce.

Serves 4 to 6   9 grams of fat per serving

Barbecue Sauce:

1	**cup catsup**	**1**	**tablespoon liquid smoke**
2	**tablespoons vinegar**	**1**	**tablespoon soy sauce**
2	**tablespoons Worcestershire sauce**	**1**	**tablespoon chile powder**

- Mix all the ingredients in a small saucepan and simmer for 15 minutes over medium heat.

Makes about 2 cups   0 grams of fat

Note: Shred any leftover brisket. Heat in a saucepan with barbecue sauce and serve in hamburger buns for a Loose Barbecue Sandwich.

Grilled Steak Kabobs

The amount of steak suggested as a serving for a low-fat diet is 4 ounces, which seems small by past standards. However, when the meat is cubed and grilled with vegetables, it seems a great plenty.

1 **pound top sirloin, trimmed**	12 **fresh mushrooms**
1¹/₂ **cups light Italian dressing**	4 **small red potatoes, cooked**
2 **tablespoons red wine**	**and halved**
1 **garlic clove, minced**	1 **green pepper, cut in chunks**
1 **teaspoon Dijon mustard**	12 **cherry tomatoes**
1 **medium red onion**	

- Cut the meat into 1-inch chunks, trimming as much fat as possible. Place in a medium-sized bowl.
- Combine 1 cup of the Italian dressing with the wine, garlic and mustard and pour over the meat. Marinate for 2 to 4 hours.
- Peel the onion and separate the layers, cutting the layers into 1¹/₂-inch pieces. Cut the mushrooms in half if they are large. Combine the vegetables in a large plastic bag. Add the remaining Italian dressing and marinate for 20 minutes, turning the bag to thoroughly coat the vegetables.
- Remove the meat and vegetables from the marinades and thread on skewers, alternating meat and vegetables. Reserve the marinade from the meat.
- Place the kabobs on the grill and cook for 4 to 5 minutes, basting with the marinade frequently; turn and grill for another 3 to 4 minutes, or until the meat is done to your preference.

Serves 4   10 grams of fat per serving

Standing Rib Roast

When a special event calls for a pink, juicy roast not usually on your menu try this easy, dependable way that works regardless of the size of the roast. The meat will be medium-rare, juicy and rich with that beef flavor Texans love. If you have roast left over, save the pan drippings for gravy for the next day. Trim all the fat and eat only a 3-ounce serving. A lean portion of choice beef will have 12 grams of fat while the same portion of prime beef will have 17.

4 - 5 pound choice standing　　　　　**Salt and pepper to taste**
　　　　rib roast

- Wipe the roast and place it in a shallow pan, ribs down. Roast, uncovered, in a preheated 350⁰ oven for 1 hour.
- Turn the oven off and leave the meat in the oven for at least 3 hours. **Do not open the oven door!**
- One and one-half hours before you are ready to serve, turn oven to 350⁰ and roast for another hour.
- Remove from the oven; season with salt and pepper.
- Allow the meat to rest for 20 minutes before carving. Deglaze the pan and reserve the pan drippings for Defatted Beef Gravy with leftovers the next day.

Serves 10　　　　14 grams of fat per 4-ounce serving

* Defatted Beef Gravy: Deglaze the pan by adding ¹/2 cup of beef broth and simmering briefly, stirring to loosen the pan drippings. Pour into a small bowl and refrigerate long enough for the fat to solidify on top; remove fat. You should have almost 1 cup of meat juices and broth. Place 2 tablespoons of flour in a heavy skillet and stir over medium heat until lightly browned. Remove from heat and gradually stir in the defatted meat juices. Return to heat and cook and stir until gravy is thickened, adding more beef broth as necessary. Salt and pepper to taste. Defatted gravy has the flavor of beef and only a trace of fat.

The mysterious lights appearing at night on the plains a few miles east of Marfa defy explanation although they have been studied by scientists, geologists, and uranium seekers. Cowboys on cattle drives back in the 1880's reported strange lights that glowed, glided and bobbed a few feet above the ground, and early settlers reported strange pulsating globes of light. Now there is seldom an evening that people aren't parked in the viewing area hoping to see this phenomena for themselves. Although weather and seasons have little effect on them, the lights are shy of people and manage to keep their distance. They are truly a Texas mystery, and maybe we don't have to have an answer for everything.

Marfa Beef Loin

Billie Christopher is the owner of La Tejana, a gift shop in a beautifully restored old hotel in Marfa. The English translation for the shop name is "the Texas woman," an apt description of Billie whose Texas flair is evident in everything she does. About this recipe, she says that an eye of the round can be substituted for the beef loin and it will be "delish."

1 3-pound beef loin	4 tablespoons soft margarine
1 cup low-sodium soy sauce	4 stems fresh dill
$^1/_2$ cup lemon juice	Freshly ground black pepper

- Trim the meat and place in a glass baking dish.
- Combine the soy sauce, lemon juice and margarine in a microwave-safe dish and microwave on High for 20 seconds, or until the margarine is melted.
- Pour the marinade over the meat. Place 2 stems of fresh dill on top of the meat and a stem on each side. Cover and refrigerate for 24 hours.
- Drain and reserve the marinade from the meat. Sprinkle with black pepper.
- Grill over medium coals, occasionally brushing with the reserved marinade, for 30 to 40 minutes, or until an instant meat thermometer reads 150^0 for medium-rare or 160^0 for medium.

Serves 6   About 12 grams of fat per 4-ounce serving

Beef and Green Chile Enchiladas

Don't think that Mexican food is not allowed when you try to lower the amount of fat you eat. For years tortillas have been dipped in oil to soften them; they're even better if they are softened for 1 minute in the microwave or heated for a few seconds in chicken broth. So many ingredients that we thought were essential to flavor aren't even missed. These enchiladas are great, and they won't hurt either your heart or your waistline.

1 **4-ounce can chopped green chilies**	1¹/₂ **pounds very lean ground beef**
1 **clove garlic, finely minced**	1 **large onion, chopped**
1 **14¹/₂-ounce can stewed tomatoes**	1 **cup light sour cream**
1 **teaspoon minced fresh oregano**	1 **cup grated Mozzarella cheese**
Salt and pepper (optional)	12 **corn tortillas**
	¹/₂ **cup chicken broth**

- Sauté the chilies, garlic, tomatoes and oregano in a medium-sized saucepan for 15 to 20 minutes, or until the sauce begins to thicken. Add salt if desired.
- While the sauce is cooking, lightly brown the ground beef and onions in a large skillet. Add the sour cream and cheese and mix gently. Salt and pepper to taste.
- Heat the chicken broth in a medium-sized saucepan. Dip the tortillas in the hot broth only long enough to make them pliable.
- Fill each tortilla with a heaping tablespoon of the beef mixture. Roll tightly and place in a baking dish. Pour the sauce over the top. Cover with foil and bake at 350⁰ for 30 minutes.

Serves 6	12 grams of fat per serving

Taco Salad

The taco salads served in restaurants can have as much as 60 grams of fat because the shells holding the salad are loaded with both fat and calories. By making your own you can have a crisp, flaky tortilla shell with greatly reduced fat and calories.

Tortilla Shells:

4 10-inch flour tortillas   **Vegetable cooking spray**

- Spray the tortillas with a light coating of cooking spray and drape each one over a small, microwave-safe mixing bowl. You may be able to do only one or two at a time unless you have several bowls of the correct size.
- Microwave on High for 30 seconds. Mold the tortillas around outside of bowl to form the shell. Cook for another 40 seconds on High. When the tortillas hold the shape of the bowls, remove them from the microwave and place on a cookie sheet. Bake the shells for 10 minutes in a 300° oven, or until lightly browned.

Taco Salad:

Vegetable cooking spray   **1   large tomato, chopped**
¹/₂ pound 95% lean ground beef   **¹/₂ avocado, chopped**
¹/₂ cup chopped onion   **2   tablespoons light Italian**
1   teaspoon chili powder   **salad dressing**
1   cup ranch style beans   **2   tablespoons mild salsa**
2   cups shredded lettuce   **¹/₂ cup shredded Mozzarella cheese**

- Coat a nonstick skillet with cooking spray. Brown the ground beef and onion until meat is no longer pink. Add the chili powder and beans and sauté briefly.
- Toss the lettuce, tomato and avocado in a large bowl. Combine the salad dressing with the salsa and pour over the vegetables. Add the meat mixture and toss; divide into the tortilla bowls. Sprinkle with the cheese and serve.

Serves 4   11 grams of fat per serving

Southwestern Stir-Fry

This easy and different way of preparing gound beef is low both in fat content and calories and is one you'll use again and again. It was one of several great recipes sent by Virginia Hughes of Gruene. She serves them with flour or corn tortillas.

1 **cup salsa**	1 **medium green pepper, cut in**
2 **teaspoons cornstarch (less if**	**1/2-inch strips**
your favorite salsa is thick)	1 **12-ounce can of corn, drained**
1 **tablespoon oil**	1 **pound very lean ground chuck**
3 **green onions, sliced**	**Tomato wedges and grated cheese**

- Combine the salsa and cornstarch and set aside.
- Place the oil in a wok or a nonstick skillet over medium-high heat. Add the onions, green pepper, and corn; cook for 3 to 4 minutes, stirring frequently. Remove the vegetables from the pan and set aside.
- Place the ground beef in the pan and cook and stir over medium-high heat until no pink remains. Drain well. Push the meat aside.
- Add the salsa and cornstarch to the pan and cook until thickened. Return the vegetables to the skillet or wok, combine with the meat and the salsa and heat.
- Serve with tomato wedges; sprinkle grated cheese over the top.

Serves 4   10 grams of fat per serving

Lone Star Chicken Fried Steak

The most frequently ordered item in restaurants throughout Texas is Chicken Fried Steak, commonly known as CFS. Certain foods are necessary to some Texans and this is one of them. Though this recipe is not truly low-fat, it lets you have your CFS fix with half the grams of fat found in the traditional method of frying the steaks in $1/2$ inch of oil.

4 4-ounce tenderized sirloin or round steaks	$1/2$ teaspoon garlic salt
$3/4$ cup egg substitute	Salt and pepper to taste
2 tablespoons low-fat milk	Vegetable cooking spray
$3/4$ cup flour	1 tablespoon vegetable oil

- Buy tenderized steaks that have been carefully trimmed.
- Combine the egg substitute and milk in a bowl and beat until thoroughly mixed.
- Combine the flour, garlic salt, salt and pepper on a plate.
- Heat a large nonstick skillet and coat with the cooking spray. Add the oil and place on medium-high heat.
- Dip the steaks into the egg mixture, then into the seasoned flour. Shake off any excess. Immediately place the meat in the skillet. Cook until browned and crusty on one side; turn carefully so as to not disturb the crust, and cook the other side. Remove from pan and drain on paper towels.

CFS Gravy:

3 tablespoons of the seasoned flour remaining on the plate	$1^1/2$ to 2 cups low-fat milk, warmed
1 tablespoon vegetable oil	Salt and pepper to taste

- Place the flour and oil in the skillet with the browned bits of meat and cook over medium heat until the flour just begins to turn a soft beige.
- Add the milk gradually and stir and cook until thickened. Add salt and pepper to taste. Pour over the steaks and serve.

Serves 4   14 grams of fat per serving

Chicken Black Bean Chile

Kelley Jemison, one of West Lake Hills' good cooks, shares an unusual and tasty chili recipe. Plan to cook the chicken the day before making the chili. When the broth is refrigerated for several hours the fat will solidify on top, making it easy to remove.

1 whole chicken	$^1/_4$ teaspoon black pepper
10 cups water	$^1/_2$ teaspoon thyme
6 whole cloves	

- Place the chicken and water in a heavy, covered saucepan. Add the seasonings and simmer for about 50 minutes, or until the meat is done.
- Allow the chicken to cool in the broth. Lift the chicken out of the broth, remove and discard the bones and the skin. Refrigerate the meat and the broth for several hours. Remove any fat that solidifies on top. Reserve the broth.

3 tablespoons margarine	1 teaspoon salt
1 red pepper, seeded and chopped	1 teaspoon oregano
1 green pepper, seeded and chopped	1 tablespoon chili powder
2 onions, chopped	$^1/_2$ teaspoon cumin
1 whole head of garlic	1 teaspoon Spike seasoning
Dash cayenne pepper	1 teaspoon basil
	$^1/_4$ teaspoon crushed red pepper

- Melt the margarine in a large nonstick skillet over medium heat. Add the peppers and onion.
- Remove the papery skin from each clove of the head of garlic. If you drop the entire head in boiling water for 1 minute and cool under cold water, the skins will slip off easily. Mince the garlic and add to the skillet.

(Continued)

Chicken Black Bean Chile (Continued)

4   16-ounce cans black beans, with liquid
2   16-ounce cans Mexican stewed tomatoes
1   10-ounce can tomato sauce

1   6-ounce can tomato paste
Reserved chicken broth
Shredded cheddar cheese
Sliced scallions or green onion tops

- Combine the beans, stewed tomatoes, tomato sauce and tomato paste in a large soup kettle.
- Shred the chicken and add to the mixture in the kettle. Add the onion and pepper mixture. Add enough chicken broth to give the chili the consistency you like. Simmer on low heat for 30 minutes.
- Serve topped with cheese and sliced scallions or green onion tops.

Serves 10 to 12   About 11 grams of fat per serving

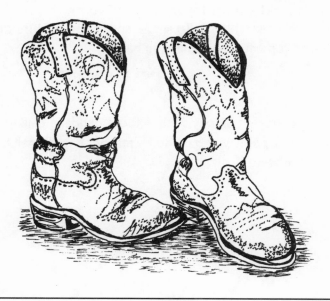

Mindy's Beef and Cabbage Joes

This variation of Sloppy Joes tastes great and can be fixed ahead.   The cabbage adds both taste and crunch. The recipe is from Mindy Walls of Fort Worth, who like many of today's fine young cooks believes in limiting the amount of fat in her cooking.

1 **pound extra-lean ground**	**³/4 cup catsup**
beef (93-95% lean)	**¹/4 cup water**
1 **medium onion, chopped**	**¹/4 teaspoon salt**
¹/2 cup thinly sliced celery	1 **tablespoon prepared mustard**
¹/3 cup chopped green pepper	8 **hamburger buns**
2 **cups shredded cabbage**	

- Brown the meat, onion, celery and green pepper in a large nonstick skillet until it is lightly browned. Drain off any fat that has accumulated in the skillet. Add the cabbage.
- Combine the catsup, water, salt and mustard; stir into the meat and vegetable mixture.
- Reduce the heat, cover and simmer for 25 minutes, stirring occasionally.
- Split and toast the hamburger buns. To serve, spoon the mixture on the bottom halves of the buns and top with the remaining halves.

Serves 8   4 grams of fat per serving

Variation: A similar version of Sloppy Joes without cabbage calls for 1 teaspoon Worcestershire sauce, 1 teaspoon vinegar and ¹/2 teaspoon garlic salt to be added to the catsup and mustard mixture.

Better-Than-Ever Meatloaf

One of our favorite meals is meatloaf served with baked potatoes and a green salad. It took several tries to develop a low-fat recipe that my husband really liked. The test of a good meatloaf is how it tastes in a sandwich the next day. Make plenty of this one because it passes the test. Look for ground beef marked "95% lean," which has 24 grams of fat per pound compared with 91 grams of fat in "80% lean" ground beef.

1 1/2 pounds extra-lean ground beef (93-95% lean)

1/2 cup chopped onion

1/4 green pepper, finely chopped

3/4 cup Quaker Oats, quick or old-fashioned

1/4 cup egg substitute

1 teaspoon dry mustard

1 tablespoon prepared horseradish

1/4 cup catsup

1/4 cup tomato juice

1 teaspoon Worcestershire sauce

1/2 teaspoon salt (optional)

1/4 teaspoon pepper

1 cup tomato sauce

- Combine all the ingredients except the tomato sauce, which is saved for the topping. Mix with your hands to thoroughly combine the ingredients.
- Shape into a loaf and place in a 9x5-inch pan.
- Spoon the tomato sauce over the top of the loaf and bake for 1 hour at 350°. Drain the fat and juices and let stand for 5 minutes before slicing and serving.

Serves 6   6 grams of fat per serving

Medallions of Pork Tenderloin

Slices of pork tenderloin combined with julienne strips of green, red and yellow bell peppers make an elegant but simple-to-prepare main course.

1	pound pork tenderloin	3	sweet peppers (red, green and yellow) cut into julienne strips
	Salt and pepper to taste		
	Vegetable cooking spray		
1	tablespoon canola oil	1	teaspoon finely minced garlic
1	medium onion, chopped	2	tablespoons chicken broth

- Cut tenderloin into eight equal slices. Flatten each slice with a meat mallet until they are about $1/2$-inch thick. Sprinkle with salt and pepper.
- Coat a large nonstick skillet with cooking spray. Add 1 teaspoon of oil and place over medium-high heat.
- When oil is hot, add the medallions and cook for 5 minutes on each side, or until browned. They are done if the juice runs clear when pierced with a fork. Remove the medallions from the skillet and set aside.
- Add the remaining 2 teaspoons of oil to the skillet over medium heat. Place the onion, peppers and garlic in the skillet and sauté over medium heat for 3 minutes, stirring constantly.
- Add the chicken broth and cook and stir for another 3 minutes.
- Spoon the peppers onto a large serving plate and arrange the medallions on top of the peppers.

Serves 4   8.5 grams of fat per serving

Barbecued Pork Chops

A well-trimmed 4-ounce loin pork chop has about 9 grams of fat and may be used on a low-fat diet. Farmers are now breeding and feeding their pigs to produce meat 31% leaner than it was a few years ago. Pork is being promoted as "the other white meat," and it adds flavor and variety to a menu. It's no wonder that people who think a low-fat diet allows them to eat only turkey and fish give up before they even start.

Hickory chips for grill
$^1/_2$ cup catsup
2 teaspoons Worcestershire sauce
2 teaspoons liquid smoke
1 teaspoon low-sodium soy sauce

1 teaspoon chile powder
Black pepper to taste
4 4-ounce pork loin chops, trimmed and cut $^1/_2$- to $^3/_4$-inch thick

- Soak the hickory chips for about 1 hour. Prepare the barbecue grill and light the fire about 30 minutes before you are ready to cook the pork chops.
- Combine the catsup, Worcestershire sauce, liquid smoke, soy sauce and chile powder in a mixing cup or small bowl.
- Rub the black pepper over the chops and brush lightly with the sauce. Bring the pork chops to room temperature; do not allow them to be unrefrigerated for more than 45 minutes.
- Add the drained hickory chips to the coals in the grill. The coals should be coated with white ash, and the cooking rack should be 6 inches above the coals. Place the chops on the grill and cook for approximately 8 minutes on one side without covering the grill.
- Turn the chops, brush the top with the sauce, cover the grill and cook and smoke for 6 to 8 minutes. Turn the chops and brush again with the sauce. Cook for another 6 minutes with the grill covered.
- Serve with the sauce.

Serves 4   About 9 grams of fat per serving

Mesquite-Grilled Pork Tenderloin

The flavcrs of mesquite and pork go well together. Add a few mesquite chips that have been soaked in water for about an hour to the charcoal before placing the tenderloin on the grill. Cook the pork quickly so it will be juicy and tender. If you use an instant meat thermometer when grilling, you can tell easily when the meat is done. Insert the stem of the thermometer into the thickest portion of the meat for only one minute to get an accurate reading.

1 1^1/$_2$ pound pork tenderloin	1 teaspoon Dijon mustard
^{1}/$_4$ cup orange juice	2 teaspoons minced garlic
^{1}/$_4$ cup low-sodium soy sauce	2 cups fresh pineapple slices
^{1}/$_2$ teaspoon ground ginger	Vegetable cooking spray

- Trim as much fat from the meat as possible. Butterfly the tenderloin by cutting lengthwise almost through. Spread the two sides and place in a heavy plastic bag.
- Combine the orange juice with the soy sauce, ginger, mustard and garlic .
- Add the marinade sauce to the meat. Close the bag securely and marinate at room temperature for 1 hour, turning occasionally.
- Remove the meat from the marinade, reserving the marinade. Coat the grill with vegetable cooking spray. Place the meat on the grill over medium coals to which a handful of wet mesquite chips has been added. Brush the meat with the marinade every 3 minutes. Cook for 7 to 8 minutes on each side, or until the meat thermometer reads 160^0. Remove from the grill and keep warm.
- Place the pineapple slices on the grill and cook for 2 to 3 minutes on each side.
- To serve, slice the tenderloin diagonally ^{1}/$_4$-inch thick. Arrange on a serving plate with the pineapple.

Serves 6   Approximately 5 grams of fat per serving

Tuna-Tomato Pita Pockets

Sun-dried tomatoes give tangy tomato flavor to this sandwich filling without the extra moisture of regular tomatoes. Capers may be substituted for the sun-dried tomatoes.

$^1/_2$ cup sun-dried tomato halves, snipped into half-inch pieces

2 6-ounce cans chunk light tuna in spring water, drained

$^1/_4$ cup diced celery

$^1/_4$ cup diced green pepper

4 green onions, minced

6 tablespoons Hellmann's Reduced Fat Mayonnaise

1 tablespoon prepared mustard

4 8-inch round pitas

1 cup shredded lettuce

- Place the sun-dried tomatoes in a medium-sized bowl. Cover with boiling water and let stand for 10 to12 minutes.
- Drain the tomatoes and pat dry with paper towels. Return them to the bowl and combine with the tuna, celery, green pepper, onions, mayonnaise and mustard. Mix well.
- Cut the round pitas in half and open the pockets.
- Spoon $^1/_4$ cup of the tuna mixture into each pita pocket. Tuck in the shredded lettuce and serve immediately.

Serves 4   5 grams of fat per serving

Dolores' Venison Chili

We met Dolores Hartley of Marshall while traveling, heard about her Venison Chili, and asked for the recipe. She says she has used this recipe for years and has never served the chile to a new group without being asked for the recipe. Venison has about half the fat content found in most cuts of beef so it is a great addition to a low-fat diet.

Vegetable cooking spray
2 tablespoons canola oil
2 pounds ground venison
2 large white onions, chopped
2 14.5-ounce cans stewed tomatoes, chopped fine
2 cups water
2 tablespoons white vinegar
2 teaspoons sugar (or 2 packets Sweet & Low sugar substitute)

2 15-ounce cans Ranch Style Beans
1 2-ounce package Mexene Chile Powder (or 2 tablespoons red chile powder and a pinch of oregano)
1 pinch cumin
$^1/_4$ teaspoon black pepper
$^1/_4$ teaspoon garlic powder
1 teaspoon salt
$^1/_4$ teaspoon cayenne pepper, (optional)

- Coat a large, heavy kettle with the cooking spray. Add the oil and place on medium heat. Add the venison and cook while stirring until the meat is no longer pink.
- Transfer the meat to another pan lined with paper towels to drain as much fat as possible. Wipe the kettle of any remaining oil or fat.
- Place the onions in a large glass measuring cup or microwave-safe bowl; cover with 2 cups of water. Microwave for 5 to 6 minutes, or until tender.
- Pour the onions and water into the kettle. Add the drained meat and the remaining ingredients.
- Bring to a boil: lower heat and simmer for 15 minutes.

Serves 10   8 grams of fat per serving

Main Events

The word "maverick" is used to describe a person who makes his own rules, someone who marches to his own beat. In early Texas, Samuel Maverick, a south Texas rancher and a signer of the Texas Declaration of Independence, did not brand his cattle which was a standard procedure on all ranches. He could then claim that any unbranded steer or calf was his. The neighboring ranchers at first thought that Maverick was not too smart, but soon realized they were losing a lot of cattle to him because of this decision. His name gave us a new and descriptive word that still fits a lot of Texans.

Dale's Quail

Houstonian Dale Culwell's business is oil but his passion is hunting, and that seems to include hunting just about anything that is legal. He cautions that timing is important when cooking quail because these tiny birds are easily overcooked. For smoking quail he uses either pecan or hickory wood or chips to enhance the flavor.

8 - 10 dressed quail	$1/2$ teaspoon garlic salt
3 cups low-fat milk	Salt and pepper to taste
$1^1/2$ cups vinegar	16 - 20 bacon slices
$1/4$ cup oil	Hickory or pecan wood or chips

- Wash the quail and place in a deep bowl or enamel pan. Cover with milk and refrigerate for several hours, or overnight. Drain and rinse.
- Prepare the marinade by combining the vinegar, oil, garlic salt, salt and pepper.
- Cover the quail with the marinade and allow to stand at room temperature for one hour.
- Prepare the smoker or grill with the wood or charcoal. If using chips, soak them in water for about an hour before adding to the coals.
- Remove the quail from the marinade and wrap a bacon strip around the top half of the bird and another around the lower half. Secure with wooden picks.
- Arrange the fire so the quail is not directly over the hot coals. Cook for 8 to 10 minutes on each side, or until done.

Serves 4 - 6   15 grams of fat per quail

Pasta with Broccoli-Tomato Sauce

Pasta, with 1 gram of fat per serving, is a perfect base for meatless meals. This sauce can be varied according to what's available. The Greek olives, freshly grated Parmesan cheese and fresh tomatoes add a wonderful Mediterranean flavor; however, black olives, Parmesan cheese from a shaker and canned Italian stewed tomatoes may be substituted.

2 cups fresh broccoli flowerets	10 Greek olives, sliced
2 large ripe tomatoes	$^{1}/_{2}$ cup coarsely chopped parsley
Vegetable cooking spray	Salt and pepper to taste
1 tablespoon olive oil	$^{1}/_{2}$ pound angel hair pasta
2 garlic cloves, minced	Freshly grated Parmesan cheese
$^{1}/_{2}$ teaspoon red pepper flakes	

- Steam the broccoli over boiling water for 3 to 4 minutes. Remove from heat and spray with cold water.
- Peel the tomatoes after immersing them in boiling water for 12 seconds. The skin will slip off easily. Chop the tomatoes coarsely.
- Coat a large nonstick skillet with the cooking spray. Add the oil and place over medium-high heat. Add the tomatoes, garlic, red pepper flakes, Greek olives, parsley, salt and pepper. Sauté for 3 to 4 minutes and add the broccoli. Cook for another 2 minutes.
- Cook the pasta according to the instructions on the package. Drain and remove to a serving plate. Ladle the sauce mixture over the pasta and sprinkle with freshly grated Parmesan cheese.

4 servings   4 grams of fat per serving

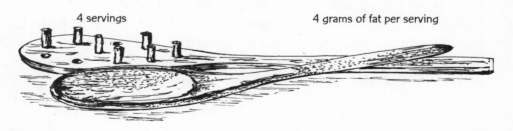

Vegetables and Side Dishes

Roadside Stand

Garden Ratatouille

The roadside stands and farmers' markets overflow with an abundance of produce during the Texas summer and fall. The combination of vegetables in this recipe is a good way to enjoy the bounty. Remember to double the recipe and freeze half; it's wonderful served over pasta or a baked potato for a quick meal. It can be served hot, cold or at room temperature and has very little fat.

1 **tablespoon canola oil**	2 **tablespoons fresh minced parsley**
2 **medium onions, sliced**	
1 **medium red pepper, chopped**	1 **teaspoon dried basil**
1 **tablespoon minced garlic**	1/2 **teaspoon dried oregano**
1 **small eggplant, cubed**	2 **large tomatoes, skinned and chopped**
3 **medium zucchini, cut into 1/2-inch slices**	
3/4 **cup canned whole tomatoes, undrained**	1/2 **teaspoon salt**
	Freshly ground black pepper

- Heat the oil in a large skillet; add the onions, red peppers and garlic; sauté for 3 minutes. Add the eggplant, zucchini, canned tomatoes, parsley, basil and oregano
- Simmer for 10 minutes, stirring occasionally. Add the remaining ingredients and simmer for another 10 minutes.

Serves 6
2.2 grams of fat per serving

Jessie's Wild Rice Casserole

We first tasted this great wild rice dish when it was served at a potluck dinner club. The friend who brought it said she got the recipe from Nancy Smith of Amarillo. I wrote Nancy asking permission to use the recipe, and it came back named for Jessie. Most of my favorite recipes have come from friends who are good cooks happy to share their recipes.

1 **4.1-ounce box Uncle Ben's Long Grain & Wild Rice**	1 **7-ounce can button mushrooms**
1 **2^1/$_4$-ounce can sliced ripe olives**	2 **tablespoons salad oil**
1 **cup grated reduced-fat Cheddar cheese**	^{1}/$_4$ **teaspoon onion salt**
2 **medium tomatoes, peeled and sliced**	1 **teaspoon salt**
	^{1}/$_4$ **teaspoon black pepper**
	1 **cup boiling water**

- Place the rice and contents of the seasoning packet in a 1^1/$_2$-quart casserole.
- Add the olives, cheese, tomatoes and mushrooms and mix. Combine the seasonings and sprinkle over the top.
- Pour the boiling water over the ingredients in the casserole and mix.
- Cover the casserole and bake for 45 minutes at 350^0. Remove the cover and bake for 15 minutes longer.

Serves 6   12 grams of fat per serving

Gerry's Special Fried Rice

Gerry Groden of Occasionally Yours Catering in Austin uses a method of preparing rice that he learned in Hong Kong, and it never fails to bring raves. The vegetables are not cooked before being added to the rice. His directions for the amount of water to use were "put enough water in the pan to cover the second knuckle of your index finger." It does work, but if you feel more comfortable with a precise measurement, one is given.

5   cups water (or enough water to cover the second knuckle of your index finger)
1   tablespoon canola oil
1   tablespoon salt
1   16-ounce box Uncle Ben's Converted Rice
2   cups finely chopped celery

1   red bell pepper, diced
6 - 8 radishes, finely chopped
6 - 8 green onions including some of the tops, sliced
1   large cucumber, peeled, seeded and finely chopped
2   tablespoons low-sodium soy sauce
2   teaspoons canola oil

- Bring the water to a boil in a large saucepan. Add the oil, salt and rice, stirring briefly to separate rice. Bring to a boil, cover and turn off the heat. Let stand until moisture is absorbed.
- Prepare the celery, red pepper, radishes and onions. Peel and seed the cucumber; chop fine. Set the vegetables aside.
- Place the soy sauce and oil in the bottom of a wok or a large nonstick skillet over medium-high heat. Fluff the rice with a fork and transfer to the wok or skillet. Stir until the rice and soy sauce are blended.
- Add the vegetables; mix and serve.

Serves 12-14   2 grams of fat per serving

Pecos Bill is the consummate Texas cowboy, and stories told about him are favorites of Texas youngsters. Pecos had a horse named Widowmaker and a girl friend named Slue-foot Sue, whom he first sighted as she was riding an enormous catfish down the Rio Grande. Pecos Bill could throw the loop of his lariat around an entire herd of cattle if he thought they were fixin' to stampede. He could even capture a lightning bolt with that same lariat if it threatened damage to the ranch where he worked. He was last heard of when he roped a Texas tornado and rode it to the ground in Arizona, where it formed the Grand Canyon. And that's the Texas truth.

Mexican Grits Casserole

Joyce Andrews grew up in the Panhandle but has lived in Houston for a long time, and the combination of west Texas and east Texas living has produced a really good cook. She is careful of the fat in her cooking and shared this recipe for Mexican Grits with us.

2^1/4 cups water
^{1}/4 teaspoon salt (optional)
^{3}/4 cups quick-cooking grits, uncooked
^{1}/2 cup shredded reduced-fat sharp Cheddar cheese
1 4-ounce can chopped green chilies, drained

1 2-ounce jar pimiento, diced and drained
1 garlic clove, crushed
^{1}/4 teaspoon hot sauce
^{1}/4 cup egg substitute
Vegetable cooking spray

- Bring the water and salt to a boil in a medium-sized saucepan. Stir in the grits; cover, reduce heat and simmer for 5 minutes, or until the mixture is thickened.
- Add the cheese, green chilies, pimiento and garlic. Stir until the cheese melts.
- Add a small amount of the grits mixture to the egg substitute and add to the remaining grits mixture, stirring constantly.
- Spoon the grits mixture into a 1-quart casserole coated with vegetable cooking spray.
- Bake at 350^0 for 30 minutes, or until set.

Serves 6   1^1/2 grams of fat per serving

Gene's Beans

*Gene Long of Houston sent this recipe to me sometime ago after using **MORE Tastes & Tales from Texas** to prepare a Texas dinner. When I wrote him for permission to put his recipe in this cookbook, his niece Katherine Hanson advised me he had died but suggested using it as a tribute. Beans with ham hocks were one of those old family dishes we considered a "comfort" food. With their high-fiber content and no fat or cholesterol, beans are wonderful for a low-fat diet; but the ham hocks listed in Gene's recipe had to go. We found that a few smoked pork chops, with only 3 grams of fat each, added flavor wiith very little fat.*

1 **pound Great Northern dried beans**	$^1/_2$ **teaspoon black pepper**
1 **medium onion, minced**	3 **smoked pork chops, trimmed**
2 **garlic cloves, minced**	2 **teaspoons salt**
2 **carrots, sliced**	1 **teaspoon brown sugar**
$^1/_2$ **cup chopped celery**	1 **tablespoon prepared mustard**

- Wash the beans and place in a large kettle with 2 quarts of water. Soak for 3 to 4 hours, or overnight.
- Drain the beans and cover with fresh water. Add the onion, garlic, carrots and celery.
- Cover and simmer slowly for 2 hours, stirring occasionally. Check the water level in the kettle, adding more as needed.
- Add the remaining ingredients and simmer for another hour, or until tender. The brown sugar does not make the beans sweet, but brings all the flavors together.

Serves 6
2 grams of fat per serving

Sweet Potato Bake with Granola Topping

4-5 large sweet potatoes
$^1/_4$ cup frozen apple juice
    concentrate
$1^1/_2$ tablespoons brown sugar
3 tablespoons non-fat buttermilk
1 teaspoon grated orange rind
Pinch of cinnamon

$^1/_2$ teaspoon salt
2 egg whites
$^1/_2$ cup low-fat granola without
    raisins, crushed
$^1/_2$ tablespoon melted margarine
2 tablespoons finely chopped pecans

- Cut the sweet potatoes in quarters and cook in boiling water for 35 to 40 minutes, or until tender; drain and let cool.
- Place the potatoes in a large bowl and, using an electric mixer, beat until mashed. Add the apple juice concentrate and beat again until smooth.
- Combine the brown sugar, buttermilk, orange rind, cinnamon and salt and stir to combine.
- Beat the egg whites with the electric mixer until stiff peaks are formed. Gently fold egg whites into the potato mixture.
- Spoon the mixture into a 2-quart casserole.
- Crush the granola with a rolling pin or in a food processor. In a small bowl, combine the granola, margarine and pecans. Sprinkle evenly over the potato mixture.
- Bake at 350° for 30 to 35 minutes.

Serves 6
5 grams of fat per serving

New Potatoes with Mushrooms

20 small new potatoes, scrubbed
2 cups fresh mushrooms
1 tablespoon olive oil
1 large clove garlic, finely minced

2 tablespoons chopped fresh parsley
2 tablespoons chopped fresh chives
1 tablespoon chopped fresh basil
Salt and pepper to taste

- Peel a narrow strip around each potato. Cut any larger potatoes in half.
- Wipe the mushrooms and trim ends of the stems. Cut larger ones in half.
- Toss the potatoes with the mushrooms, oil and garlic in a medium-sized bowl using your hands to coat evenly. Mix in the herbs, salt and pepper.
- Place the mixture in a 3-quart baking dish. Bake at 350^0 for 45 minutes or until potatoes are tender.

Serves 8   2 grams of fat per serving

Sliced Oven-Roasted Potatoes

4 medium-sized baking potatoes
Vegetable cooking spray
$^1/2$ teaspoon Knorr's Seasoning

2 teaspoons dried parsley
1 tablespoon margarine, melted
2 tablespoons grated Parmesan cheese

- Scrub the potatoes and slice $^1/4$-inch thick.
- Coat a glass baking dish with cooking spray. Place the potato slices so they overlap each other about half the width of the slice.
- Sprinkle the slices with the Knorr's Seasoning and dried parsley. Drizzle with the margarine. Bake at 425^0 for 45 minutes.
- Remove from the oven and sprinkle with the Parmesan cheese. Return to the oven and bake for another 10 minutes.

Serves 4   5 grams of fat per

Dot's Country Potatoes

Green peppers, tomatoes, cheese and mushrooms combine to add color and flavor to potatoes for a delicious and attractive dish that can be prepared ahead of time. The recipe is from Dot Fields of Lakeway who is one of the best cooks I know.

8 medium potatoes, unpeeled
Vegetable cooking spray
1 green pepper, chopped
1 medium onion, chopped
1 tablespoon margarine
1 cup stewed tomatoes

1 3-ounce can sliced
   mushrooms
Salt and pepper to taste
$^1/_2$ cup shredded sharp
   Cheddar cheese

- Cut the cooked, unpeeled potatoes into $^3/_4$-inch chunks and place in a 2-quart casserole.
- Coat a nonstick skillet with cooking spray. Add the margarine and melt over medium heat. Add the green pepper and onion and sauté until transparent. Spread over the potatoes.
- Add the tomatoes, mushrooms and seasonings, mixing gently.
- Top with the shredded cheese, cover with aluminum foil and bake at 350° for 25 minutes.
- Remove the foil and bake for another 20 minutes, or until potatoes and cheese are lightly browned.

Serves 8   6.5 grams of fat per serving

Low-Fat Scalloped Potatoes

6 medium potatoes, sliced
 $^1/_4$-inch thick
Salt and pepper to taste
2 tablespoons minced onion

$^1/_3$ cup Cream Sauce Base (page 160)
$1^1/_4$ cups water
$^1/_4$ cup grated Cheddar cheese
2 tablespoons bread crumbs

- Place half of the potatoes in a small casserole; add salt, pepper and half of the onion.
- Mix the Cream Sauce Base with the water and microwave on High for 4 minutes, stirring after 2 minutes. Cream Sauce Base should be thickened.
- Pour half of the sauce over the potatoes in the casserole. Sprinkle half of the grated cheese over the sauce.
- Repeat the process with the remaining potatoes, onion and sauce.
- Mix the bread crumbs with the rest of the cheese and sprinkle on top.
- Cover casserole and bake at 350° for 40 minutes. Remove cover and bake for another 30 minutes, or until the potatoes are tender.

Serves 4-6
3 grams of fat per serving

Not-To-Worry Fried Potatoes

These have the taste and the crunch you want in fried potatoes, but little of the fat. Potatoes are especially good for someone on a low-fat diet because they have only a trace of fat and they do fill you up .

4 - 5 medium-sized potatoes, cooked and cooled	**1/2 teaspoon dried rosemary**
2 tablespoons oil	**1 teaspoon salt**
1/2 cup finely chopped onion	**1/2 teaspoon black pepper**
	Vegetable cooking spray

- Slice the potatoes into a large bowl. Add 1/2 tablespoon oil, chopped onion, dried rosemary, salt and pepper. Toss to mix thoroughly.
- Coat a large nonstick skillet with cooking spray. Heat the remaining oil in the skillet and add the potato mixture. Cook over moderately high heat for 10-12 minutes, turning occasionally, until potatoes and onions are nicely browned.

Serves 4   7 grams of fat per serving

Microwave Baked Potatoes

For a quick lunch or light supper, top these potatoes with low-fat sour cream, reduced-fat cheese or the following sauce. The time required to bake the potatoes varies according to the size and number you are cooking.

4 medium-large baking potatoes	**1/2 cup chopped green pepper**
Vegetable cooking spray	**2 garlic cloves**
1/2 cup chopped onion	**1 14 1/2-ounce can stewed tomatoes**

- Wash the potatoes, prick with a fork and wrap in a damp paper towel. Microwave for 16 to 20 minutes, or until they are tender.
- Coat a nonstick skillet with cooking spray and place over medium heat. Add the onion, green pepper and garlic; sauté for 3 minutes. Add the stewed tomatoes and simmer briefly. Ladle over the opened baked potatoes.

Serves 4   1 grams of fat per serving

Garden Roundup Vegetables

The vegetables in a stir-fry may vary according to the season and what's available in the refrigerator, but it seems the flavors always blend and complement each other.

Vegetable cooking spray
1 large carrot cut in julienne strips
6 green onions, sliced
1 cup fresh sugar snap peas, trimmed

$1/2$ sweet red pepper cut in $1/2$-inch strips
1 large rib of celery, thinly sliced
$1/2$ cup sliced mushrooms
$1/4$ cup chicken broth
Salt and pepper to taste

- Coat a large nonstick skillet with the cooking spray. Heat until the skillet is hot but not smoking.
- Add the carrot strips and onions and stir-fry for 3 minutes. Add the peas, red pepper and celery and stir-fry for another 3 minutes.
- Add the mushrooms and chicken broth. Cover the skillet and cook for about 2 minutes, or until vegetables are tender but still crisp.
- Season to taste. Serve immediately.

Serves 4   Less than 1 gram of fat per serving

Broiled Parmesan Tomatoes

When tomatoes are broiled briefly they remain firm, and the heat accentuates their flavor. Fresh olive oil is a wonderful addition to salads and vegetables, because of its flavor and because it is monounsaturated, which makes it more effective in reducing blood cholesterol levels. Red wine has been given credit for the lower incidence of heart attacks in the French and Italians even though they consume higher levels of fat. Their use of olive oil in their cooking is probably a more important factor than their intake of wine.

4   medium tomatoes
Vegetable cooking spray
Salt and pepper to taste
3   tablespoons dry bread crumbs
2   tablespoons Parmesan cheese

2   tablespoons chopped parsley
$^1/_2$ teaspoon garlic powder
2   teaspoons finely chopped fresh basil
1 $^1/_2$ tablespoons olive oil

- Wash the tomatoes; cut off and discard the tops. Slice the tomatoes in half; coat with vegetable spray. Salt and pepper to taste.
- Combine the remaining ingredients and sprinkle over the cut surface of the tomatoes.
- Place on a cookie sheet or broiler pan. Broil for 3 minutes, or until the cheese mixture is lightly browned.

Serves 8   3 grams of fat per serving

Easy Corn on the Cob

For cooking small batches of corn on the cob, no method is easier than microwaving; and the corn retains more flavor and crispness than when cooked by other means. Plan on 2 to 3 minutes for each ear of corn; less time if the corn is very tender, a little more if it's not as fresh. Also, buy corn in the husks because the husks help retain flavor and freshness.

4 large ears of corn,   **1 teaspoon water**
husks and silks removed

- Place the corn in a microwave-safe dish. Add water and cover with waxed paper or plastic wrap. Pierce the covering in several places.
- Microwave on High for 8 to 10 minutes. Let stand in the microwave for 1 minute to complete cooking.
- Remove the covering carefully to prevent being scalded by the steam.

Serves 4   0 grams of fat per serving

Variation: **Unhusked Corn on the Cob:** Many corn lovers believe that when corn is microwaved while still in the husks it has more natural flavor. Just remove any of the outer husks that are wilted or soiled and follow the instructions given above. The silks will pull away easily when the husks are removed.

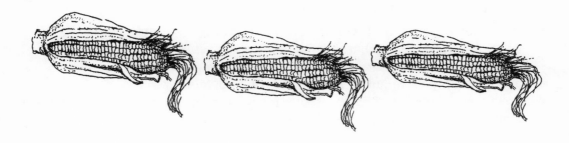

Vegetable Medley

*My favorite cooking class was one given by Jean Durkee, author of **Tout de Suite a la Microwave I and Tout de Suite a la Microwave II,** two best-selling cookbooks featuring gourmet cooking in the microwave oven. With her permission, I'm passing along this beautiful way to serve vegetables that was featured in her second book.*

1/2 **head cauliflower, cut into flowerets**	2 **medium onions, quartered**
1/2 **bunch broccoli, cut into flowerets**	6 **whole Brussels sprouts**
1 **(12-ounce) bag medium carrots, sliced round or in sticks**	4 **large whole mushrooms**
1 **yellow squash, sliced round**	1 **green or red bell pepper, cut in rings**
1 **zucchini, sliced round or in sticks**	1/4 **cup margarine, melted**
	1 to 2 **teaspoons Morton Nature's Seasons or Jane's Krazy Mixed-up salt**

- Arrange rinsed and prepared vegetables on a 12-inch glass plate in an attractive, colorful way with the harder vegetables (cauliflower, broccoli and carrots) on the outer edge of plate.
- Place the softer vegetables (squash and zucchini) in the center of plate, with onions, Brussels sprouts and mushrooms midway between the outer and center circles.
- Place slices of bell pepper on top. Do not season or add water.
- Cover tightly with thin plastic wrap (will take two sheets). Do not puncture.
- Microwave on High (100%) for 10 minutes. Check vegetables for doneness (test carrots), remembering to lift wrap away from you.
- Cook for an additional 2 minutes for softer vegetables. Cooking time is approximately 5 minutes per pound of vegetables.
- Drain liquid from vegetables, reserve for soup or gravy, and pour or squeeze margarine over cooked vegetables. Sprinkle with seasoned salt.

Serves 8   5.5 grams fat per serving

The grocery store clerk was asked where the powdered wine could be found. When the clerk said he didn't know there was such a thing, the woman said, "There must be because my recipe calls for dry white wine." We asume this was not in Texas.

Pepper Medley

This stir-fry adds both color and flavor to lamb, pork or beef and can be served over the meat or as a side dish. It takes a simple dish from the ordinary to the special.

1 large sweet red pepper	Vegetable cooking spray
1 large green pepper	1 tablespoon vegetable oil
1 large yellow pepper	2 tablespoons dry white wine
1 large red onion	1 teaspoon fresh minced basil

- Remove the core and seeds from the peppers and cut into strips about $1/4$-inch wide and 2 inches long. Slice the onion and cut the slices in half.
- Coat a nonstick skillet with cooking spray and add the oil. Place over medium-high heat until hot.
- Add the peppers and onion and stir-fry for 2 minutes. Add the wine and fresh basil, cover and cook for another 2 minutes.

Serves 4 to 6 $3 1/2$ grams of fat per serving

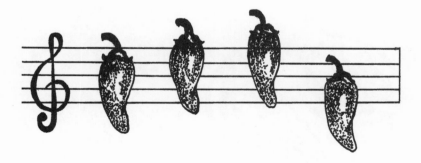

Black-Eyed Peas with Okra

Fresh black-eyed peas and okra served with golden cornbread are one of those combinations Yankees don't get too excited about. But for me they bring back memories of sitting on the back porch at my grandmother's house, helping her shell the peas.

1 quart fresh black-eyed peas	**2 medium tomatoes, sliced**
1 teaspoon salt	**2 cups okra, sliced**
2 medium onions, thinly sliced	**Salt and pepper to taste**

- Shell and wash the peas, saving a few of the hulls and tender young snaps. Place the peas, hulls and snaps in a large saucepan. Cover with water, add the salt and quickly bring to a boil. Reduce the heat and cook for 30 minutes, or until tender.
- Drain the peas, saving 1 cup of the pot liquor.
- Place the peas and the reserved pot liquor in the bottom of a large saucepan.
- Layer the onion, tomatoes and okra on top of the peas. Cook over low heat for 10 to 15 minutes, until the okra is tender.
- Serve with cornbread and big glasses of iced tea.

Serves 4-6   1 gram of fat per serving

Along one of the Hill Country roads southwest of Hunt there's a stretch of fence deco-rated with hard-used boots that has been dubbed "The Boot Fence." It all started when a local rancher kept finding boots belonging to his neighbor's six sons on his doorstep. As a joke, he stuck them on his fence posts. Soon other neighbors decided that was just the place for their most dilapidated boots and they added to those already there. A count taken a while back had over 200 pieces of worn footware strung along a considerable portion of the road.

Two-Squash Stir-Fry

4 small yellow summer squash	$1/2$ tablespoon vegetable oil
4 small zucchini	$1/2$ teaspoon fresh basil
$1/2$ sweet red pepper	1 clove garlic, finely minced
$1/2$ medium onion	Parmesan cheese
Vegetable cooking spray	Chopped parsley

- Diagonally slice the yellow squash and the zucchini about $1/8$-inch thick.
- Cut the red pepper into 3-to 4-inch-long julienne strips. Slice the onion rings.
- Coat a large nonstick skillet with the cooking spray, add the oil and place over medium-high heat until hot.
- Add the vegetables, basil and garlic. Cook and stir for 4 to 5 minutes, until the squash is tender but still crisp. Sprinkle with Parmesan cheese and parsley.

Serves 6   About 1 gram of fat per serving

Matchstick Zucchini and Carrots

Because the vegetables are cut into julienne strips, they cook quickly and taste especially fresh. Choose the long, firm zucchini -- they are usually crisper and have fewer seeds than the chunkier ones.

2 medium zucchini, unpeeled
4 medium carrots, peeled
Vegetable cooking spray
1 tablespoon olive oil
2 tablespoons chicken broth

1 teaspoon lemon juice
1 teaspoon chopped fresh dill
Salt and pepper (optional)
Fresh dill sprigs

- Cut the zucchini and carrots lengthwise into slices $^1/_4$-inch thick. Stack the slices and cut into $^1/_4$-inch strips about 3 inches long. Set strips aside.
- Coat a nonstick skillet with vegetable spray. Add the oil and place over medium heat. Add the carrots and sauté for 1 minute.
- Add the chicken broth and simmer briefly. Add the zucchini, lemon juice, dill and seasonings. Cover; cook for 3 minutes, or until vegetables are tender but still crisp.
- Salt and pepper to taste. Serve warm, garnished with sprigs of fresh dill.

Serves 6   2.5 grams of fat per serving

Texas has the Davis Mountains, the plains of the Panhandle, the desert of West Texas, the tall pine forests of East Texas, the farms of the Blackland Belt, the lakes and hills of the Hill Country and the wide sandy beaches of the Gulf Coast. Author Mary Lasswell expressed her wonder at the changing landscapes of Texas by reasoning, "I am forced to conclude that God made Texas on his day off, for pure entertainment, just to prove what diversity could be crammed into one section of earth by a really top hand."

Cumin Zucchini Stir-Fry

Dennis Burdette of Carrollton is an adventurous cook who comes up with some great re-cipes. It seems that men are more likely to take risks when cooking and women stay with known ingredients and methods . The next time you have zillions of zucchini, try this Italian squash cooked in an oriental style with a Southwest flavor.

2	large zucchini	1	teaspoon brown sugar
1	tablespoon canola oil	1	teaspoon red wine vinegar
2	teaspoons ground cumin	3	tablespoons white wine

- Wash zucchini and slice into 1-inch pieces. Cut each slice into fourths.
- Heat a Chinese wok or a large nonstick skillet over medium-high heat; add the cooking oil and the zucchini to the hot pan. Stir-fry for 30 seconds. Add the cumin and stir-fry for 1 minute.
- Combine the brown sugar, vinegar and white wine; add to the zucchini. Stir-fry for another 30 seconds.
- Remove to a serving bowl and pour the pan juices over the top.

Serves 4   3 grams of fat per serving

Vegetables and Side Dishes

Mustang Island, with its beautiful beaches and sunshine, is a favorite vacation retreat for Texans. A quick ferryboat ride takes you from the mainland to this barrier island situated between Corpus Christi Bay and the Gulf of Mexico. Life slows down when your main activity is walking the beach and maybe going fishing. If going fishing is too strenuous, you can always just watch the fishing boats come in. And when you get hungry, there are dozens of interesting restaurants featuring seafood just off the boat and other in-house specialties.

Mustang Island Black Bean Relish
as created by Bill Stephens for Pelican's Landing Restaurant, Port Aransas, Texas

Our favorite restaurant on Mustang Island is Pelican's Landing, which offers traditional Texas Coast fare as well as its own original dishes blending Mexican and Cajun influences. One of the most intriguing items, which is served with several of their entrées, is this black bean, mango, jicama relish.

1/2 **pound black beans**	1/2 **jicama, peeled and diced into**
1 **quart water**	**1/4-inch cubes**
1 **tablespoon chicken base**	1 **large tomato, peeled and finely**
1/2 **tablespoon black pepper**	**chopped**
1/2 **medium onion, finely diced**	1 **mango, peeled and finely diced**
1/2 **choyote squash, peeled, seeded**	**(bottled mangoes may be substituted)**
and diced into 1/4-inch cubes	1/3 **cup whole-kernel corn, drained**
2 **tablespoons finely chopped**	1/4 **cup sweet-pickle juice**
cilantro	1 **tablespoon cider vinegar**

- Place the black beans in a large saucepan; add the water, chicken base and black pepper. Bring to a rolling boil, cover and set aside. Let cool to room temperature.
- Bring to a boil a second time, adding more water if necessary. Cook until the beans are tender but still whole. Let them cool; drain and rinse well.
- Add the remaining ingredients except for pickle juice and vinegar. Combine the pickle juice and vinegar, pour over the relish and mix thoroughly but gently.
- Refrigerate for several hours to allow the flavors to blend.

Makes 6 cups   Only a trace of fat per serving

Creamy Baked 1015 Onions

Texas 1015 onions are wonderfully mild, sweet onions grown in the Rio Grande Valley. Their name comes from the date the onions are planted, October 15th. Because the days are short during the growing season, the onions have less acidity than those grown in the long, hot days of summer. In taste tests of the Texas 1015, the Vidalia onion of Georgia and the Walla-Walla of Washington, the Texas onion wins again and again. Onions are usually used to enhance other flavors, but this dish makes the onion the culinary star.

4 **large Texas 1015 onions**
2 **tablespoons margarine**
2 **garlic cloves, minced**
1 **cup chicken broth**
1 **packet Lipton's Cream of Chicken Cup-a-Soup Mix**

$^1/_4$ **cup grated Parmesan cheese**
2 **teaspoons sodium-reduced soy sauce**
$^1/_2$ **teaspoon black pepper**
$^1/_2$ **cup seasoned bread crumbs**

- Peel and slice the onions. Separate some of the slices into rings.
- Reserve 1 tablespoon of margarine for the topping. Place 1 tablespoon of margarine, the garlic, the chicken broth and the contents of the packet of soup mix in a large saucepan; stir. Add the onion rings and simmer until tender.
- Transfer the onion rings to a 2-quart casserole leaving some of the broth mixture in the pan. Mix the Parmesan cheese, soy sauce and pepper with the broth mixture and pour over the onions.
- Melt the reserved margarine and mix with the bread crumbs.
- Sprinkle the bread crumb mixture over the top of the onion mixture and bake at 350^0 for 30 minutes.

Serves 6   4.2 grams of fat per serving

NEW TASTES of Texas

Sweets
and Treats

Gruene

Lake Travis Pavlova

When Ann and Cole Rowland were in New Zealand recently, they were served Pavlova on board their ship, in hotels and at private homes. They enjoyed it and brought the recipe back to Texas. Ann and I revised the recipe to get it "as light as the Russian ballerina was on her feet." As with most meringues it is best prepared on a sunny day when the humidity is low. It is a delightful low-fat dessert and beautiful to serve.

Vegetable cooking spray	1 teaspoon vanilla
4 egg whites	Whipped topping (Cool-Whip or
Pinch of cream of tartar	Reddi wip Lite)
$^1/_4$ teaspoon salt	3 kiwi fruit, peeled and thinly sliced
1 scant cup of sugar	2 cups strawberries, sliced
1 teaspoon white vinegar	

- Preheat the oven to 300^0. Line a 9-inch springform pan with wax paper and coat with cooking spray.
- Combine the egg whites, cream of tartar and salt in a large mixing bowl. Using an electric mixer, beat until foamy and frothy.
- Beating at medium speed, add about 2 tablespoons of sugar per minute until stiff peaks form. Add the vinegar and vanilla to the egg whites and beat at high speed until they are glossy and stiff, or until "they won't fall out of the bowl" as they say in New Zealand.
- Spoon mixture into the prepared pan. Place in oven and bake for 50 minutes. Turn the oven off, but leave the Pavlova in the oven for another 25 minutes. Remove from the oven and cool. Very gently run a thin knife around the edge of the pan to loosen the meringue. Release the sides of the springform pan, careully remove the wax paper from the bottom and transfer to a serving plate.
- When ready to serve, swirl the whipped topping over the meringue and decorate with the kiwi and strawberries.

Serves 6   About 3 grams of fat per serving

Melva's Raspberry-Lemon Bombe

An elegant dessert that is simple to make is a real treasure, and this jewel comes from my elegant friend Melva Ribe. A variation is to use peach sherbet or yogurt instead of lemon yogurt. Then you will have Melva's Peach Melba Bombe. Sherbet, sorbet and yogurt can be interchanged as ingredients in this recipe.

2 **cups low-fat granola**	**¹/2 cup seedless red raspberry preserves**
2 **tablespoons melted margarine**	
1 **quart frozen fat-free lemon yogurt or sherbet, divided**	1 **pint frozen fat-free raspberry yogurt or raspberry sherbet**

- Combine the granola and melted margarine; Pat about ¹/4 of the crumbs in the bottom of a 6-cup bombe mold or a 2-quart mixing bowl that has been lined with clear plastic wrap. Place the crumb-lined bowl in the freezer for 15 minutes.
- Remove half the lemon yogurt from the freezer so it has about 15 minutes to soften. When softened enough to stir, spoon evenly into the crumb-lined bowl.
- Gently spread half the raspberry preserves on top of the yogurt to within ¹/2 inch of the edge. Sprinkle with 4 tablespoons of the crumb mixture.
- Return to the freezer for about 20 minutes, or until firm. Remove the raspberry yogurt from the freezer to soften.
- Spread the raspberry yogurt over the frozen mixture. Add the remaining preserves and another 4 tablespoons of the crumb mixture.
- Place the mixture in the freezer again until firm. Spoon the remaining lemon yogurt over the mixture and sprinkle the rest of the crumbs on top.
- Freeze for at least 4 hours. Unmold onto a serving plate a few minutes before serving.
- Cut into 10 servings and serve with Crimson Raspberry Sauce (see page 159).

Serves 10   3 grams of fat per serving.

Sweets and Treats

The Inn on the Creek in Salado is nestled along the bank of the Salado Creek and offers unsurpassed hospitality and food. The original structure dates to the 1890's and, with its annexes and a guest cottage, offers the comfortable elegance of a Victorian inn. Where an old trail crosses the creek nearby, you can still see ruts from wagons and stagecoaches from long ago when the area was a favorite stopping place. Now Salado is a favorite stopover for people sampling the quality of life of this pretty little town.

Strawberry Champagne Sorbet

Suzi Epps of the Inn on the Creek sent this recipe for a delicious sorbet, an example of the elegant food served there. She mentioned that she has used frozen unsweetened strawberries when fresh ones were not available.

1 1/2 **cups champagne**
1 1/2 **cups sugar**

6 **cups fresh strawberries**
1 1/2 **tablespoons lemon juice**

- Combine the champagne and the sugar; boil until the sugar dissolves, stirring occasionally. Boil for 3 minutes without stirring. Remove from the heat and allow to cool.
- Reserve a few strawberries for garnish. Place the remaining strawberries and lemon juice in a food processor or blender and purée until smooth.
- Stir the purée into the champagne mixture. Pour into a 2-quart electric freezer.
- Freeze according to the manufacturer's instructions. Let ripen for 1 hour.
- Scoop the sorbet into dessert bowls and top with the reserved strawberries.

Serves 12

Less than 1/2 gram of fat per serving

Plyl's Glazed Lemon Bundt Cake

When our family gathers, food is usually involved and everyone brings something. We all ask my sister-in-law Phyllis Hook to bring this family favorite. She converted a recipe found on a box of Duncan Hines cake mix to lower the fat and cholesterol. The Lemon Glaze with the lemon zest keeps the cake from being too sweet. Everyone raves about the cake and it's simple to make.

1 **box Duncan Hines Lemon Supreme Cake Mix**	$^1/_3$ **cup canola oil**
1 **3.4-ounce box lemon instant pudding mix**	1 **cup water**
	1 **cup egg substitute**

- Blend the cake ingredients in a large bowl. Mix, using an electric mixer, for 2 minutes at medium speed.
- Pour the mixture into a bundt pan that has been coated generously with cooking spray and dusted with flour.
- Bake in a preheated 350⁰ oven for 50 minutes, or until a toothpick inserted in the center comes out clean.
- Cool for 30 minutes. Invert pan and carefully remove the cake from the pan.
- Make the Lemon Glaze from the recipe below and spread on the cake while it is slightly warm.

Lemon Glaze:

1 $^1/_2$ **tablespoons lemon juice**	$^3/_4$ **cup sifted powdered sugar**
1 **teaspoon grated lemon rind**	

- Combine the ingredients and mix until smooth. The mixture will be thinner than a frosting.
- Spoon the glaze over the top of the cake, letting it run down the sides.

Serves 16   8 grams of fat per serving

Lemma's Chocolate Cake

Lemma Nite of San Marcos is a dedicated cookbook collector who has over 5,800 on the bookshelves in her house. Cookbooks may be short on plot but they are her favorite bedtime reading. Unlike some collectors, she uses hers by trying one or two new recipes every week. She sent this one for a heart-healthy chocolate cake that is silky in texture and great to eat.

1³/₄ cups sifted cake flour	1 cup skim milk
2 cups sugar	¹/₂ cup corn oil
¹/₂ cup cocoa	¹/₂ cup egg substitute
1¹/₂ teaspoons baking powder	1 tablespoon vanilla
1¹/₂ teaspoons baking soda	1 cup boiling water
¹/₂ teaspoon salt	Vegetable cooking spray

- Preheat the oven to 350⁰.
- Sift the flour, sugar, cocoa, baking powder, soda and salt together into a large mixing bowl.
- Add the milk, oil, egg substitute and vanilla and mix with an electric mixer on medium speed for 2 minutes.
- Add the boiling water and mix thoroughly. The batter will be thinner than most cake batters.
- Spray a 9x13-inch baking pan with vegetable spray and dust with flour. Pour the batter into the pan and bake for 30 to 40 minutes, or until the cake tests done when a wooden pick is inserted in the center

Frosting:

4 tablespoons margarine	2 cups powdered sugar, sifted
3¹/₂ tablespoons skim milk	¹/₂ teaspoon vanilla

- Bring the margarine and the milk to a boil. Remove from the heat and add the powdered sugar and vanilla.
- Mix and spread on the warm cake.

Makes 16 pieces   10 grams of fat per piece

Panhandle Carrot Cake

The recipe for this rich, moist cake with a wonderful Orange Cream Frosting comes from Sue Kidd of Amarillo.

3 cups finely shredded carrots	1/4 teaspoon ground nutmeg
1 cup shredded sweetened coconut	1/2 cup honey
1/2 cup drained crushed pineapple	1/2 cup firmly packed light brown sugar
2 cups all-purpose flour	
2 teaspoons baking soda	1 cup plain low-fat yogurt
1 teaspoon ground cinnamon	1/2 cup vegetable oil
1/2 teaspoon baking powder	2 eggs
1/2 teaspoon salt	2 egg whites
1/4 teaspoon ground allspice	1 teaspoon vanilla

- Combine the carrots, coconut and pineapple in a medium-sized bowl.
- Combine the flour, baking soda, cinnamon, baking powder, salt, allspice and nutmeg in a large bowl.
- Whisk together the honey, brown sugar, yogurt, oil, eggs, egg whites and vanilla in a large bowl until well blended. Add to the flour mixture, whisking until smooth. Add the carrot mixture, stirring only until thoroughly combined.
- Divide the mixture evenly between two oiled 9-inch-round cake pans.
- Bake in a preheated 350° oven for 35 minutes, or until a wooden toothpick inserted in the center comes out clean. Remove pans to wire racks and cool for 10 minutes. Invert the cakes onto the wire racks to cool completely.

Orange Cream Frosting:

1/2 cup margarine, softened	1/4 cup orange juice
1/4 teaspoon salt	2 tablespoons grated orange rind
3 3/4 cups powdered sugar	

- Beat margarine and salt until fluffy. Add the powdered sugar and orange juice alternately, beating after each addition until mixture is smooth. Fold in the grated orange rind and mix.
- Spread the frosting on one layer, top with the second layer and spread over all.

Serves 12   16 grams of fat per serving

Sweets and Treats

A bunch of the boys were arguing about "who's the best" back in 1883 in Pecos, Texas, so the cowboys from the Hashknife and other local ranches spent an afternoon roping and riding and wrangling. and the rodeo was born. The exceptional West of the Pecos Museum, located in the building that was once the Orient Hotel, commemorates this event as well as other significant happenings in the history of the life of this railroad and cow country town. The name of the museum comes from the days when Judge Roy Bean was known as the "Law West of the Pecos," that vast, untamed part of Texas spreading west of the Pecos River.

Pecos Cantaloupe-Strawberry Parfait

The combination of hot sun, dry air and alkaline soil are the special ingredients that gives that wonderful, sweet flavor to Pecos cantaloupes. The Texas & Pacific Railroad first introduced the melons to the rest of the world by serving them in railway dining cars; and Pecos cantaloupes were soon being shipped throughout the country. This recipe is from the West of the Pecos Museum.

1 large cantaloupe, cut into balls	$^1/_4$ teaspoon cinnamon
1 pint strawberries, cut in halves	1 tablespoon rum or $^1/_2$
$^1/_2$ cup sugar	teaspoon rum extract
$^1/_4$ cup water	6 sprigs mint
$^1/_2$ cup clover honey	

- Alternate layers of strawberries and melon balls in 6 parfait glasses.
- Place the sugar and water in a small saucepan and boil over medium-high heat until the syrup spins a thread or, if you use a candy thermometer, the temperature reaches 230°.
- Combine the honey, cinnamon and rum; stir into the syrup. Cool.
- Pour about 2 tablespoons of the syrup over the fruit in each parfait glass. Decorate with sprigs of mint.

Serves 6   0 grams of fat per serving

Medina Apple Crisp

Medina, which is west of San Antonio and a few miles from Bandera, is the apple capital of Texas. More and more apples are grown every year in Texas, and most of them are the tart, crisp varieties that are good for baking. This simple, satisfying dessert is especially good when served while still warm from the oven.

6 - 7 tart apples, pared and sliced	**1 teaspoon cinnamon**
1 tablespoon lemon juice	**1 cup quick-cooking oats**
$^1/_4$ cup sugar	**$^1/_3$ cup brown sugar**
Pinch of salt	**$^1/_2$ cup flour**
	3 tablespoons melted margarine

- Spread the apple slices in a 9x9-inch baking pan and sprinkle with the lemon juice, sugar, salt and cinnamon.
- Combine the oats, brown sugar, flour and margarine and spread over the apple filling.
- Bake at 350⁰ for 35 to 40 minutes, or until the fruit is bubbly and the topping is lightly browned.

Serves 7   4.7 grams of fat per serving

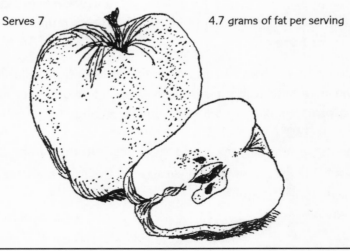

Peach-Blueberry Crisp

6 cups sliced fresh peaches
2 cups fresh blueberries
2 teaspoons lemon juice
1 teaspoon almond extract
1/3 cup brown sugar, packed
2 tablespoons all-purpose flour
1 teaspoon cinnamon

Topping:
1 cup quick-cooking rolled oats, uncooked
1 teaspoon cinnamon
1/4 cup brown sugar, packed
3 tablespoons melted butter

- Place the peaches, blueberries, lemon juice and almond extract in a medium-sized bowl. Combine the brown sugar. flour and cinnamon; add to fruit and mix.
- Turn the mixture into a 9x9-inch baking dish.
- Make the topping by combining the oats, cinnamon, brown sugar and melted margarine.
- Sprinkle over the top of the fruit mixture. Bake in 375° oven for 25 minutes, or until the top is golden brown and the fruit is bubbly. Serve warm or cold.

Serves 8

5 grams of fat per serving

Margie's Chocolate Amaretto Cheesecake

Margie Barnes of Lakeway insists she's really not a cook, but every time she entertains the food is very special. Her cheesecake tastes deliciously rich, although it has very little fat.

$^1/_4$ cup chocolate wafer crumbs,
    finely crushed (about 7 wafers)
Vegetable cooking spray
1 cup sugar
1$^1/_2$ cups Neufchatel cheese
1 cup low-fat cottage cheese
6 tablespoons unsweetened cocoa
$^1/_4$ cup all-purpose flour
$^1/_4$ cup amaretto

$^1/_4$ teaspoon salt
$^1/_4$ cup egg substitute
1 teaspoon vanilla extract
3 tablespoons semi-sweet
    chocolate mini-morsels
Crimson Raspberry Sauce
    (see page 159)
Fresh Raspberries

- Spread the chocolate wafer crumbs evenly in the bottom of an 8-inch springform pan coated with cooking spray. Set aside.
- Combine the sugar, cheeses, cocoa, flour and amaretto in the bowl of a blender or food processor. Process until smooth. Add the salt, egg substiture and vanilla; blend only until combined.
- Fold in the chocolate morsels. Pour the mixture over the crumbs in the pan.
- Bake at 300° for 50 to 60 minutes, or until the cheese cake is set. Let the cake cool before removing from the pan.
- Chill for at least 8 hours. Just before serving, spread the Crimson Raspberry Sauce over the cheesecake and garnish with fresh raspberries.

Serves 12   7$^1/_2$ grams of fat per serving

Café au Lait Cheesecake

For you cheesecake lovers, here is a wonderful one with a lot less fat and calories than most from Karen Crager of Houston.

Cheesecake Crust:

Vegetable cooking spray

3 tablespoons Grape-Nuts cereal

1 tablespoon chopped walnuts

1 tablespoon sugar

- Coat a 9-inch springform pan with vegetable cooking spray. Combine the cereal, walnuts and sugar in the bowl of a food processor and process until fine.
- Sprinkle the crumb mixture in the prepared pan; tilt pan and tap sides to evenly coat the bottom and sides with the crumbs.

Cheesecake Filling:

2^1/$_2$ tablespoons instant coffee

2^1/$_2$ tablespoons Kahlúa (or other coffee-flavored liqueur)

16 ounces low-fat cottage cheese, drained

12 ounces light sour cream

12 ounces light cream cheese

^{1}/$_8$ teaspoon ground cinnamon

^{1}/$_2$ cup sugar

6 tablespoons all-purpose flour

2 large eggs

2 large egg whites

1^1/$_2$ tablespoons cocoa

Chocolate curls or candied coffee beans for garnish

- Dissolve the instant coffee in the coffee-flavored liqueur in a cup and set aside.
- Place the cottage cheese in a food processor and process until very smooth. Add the remaining ingredients, except garnish, and process until blended.
- Pour the batter into the prepared pan and bake in a preheated 300° oven for 1 hour, or until firm around the edges but not set in the center. Turn the oven off, leaving the cheesecake inside with the door closed for 30 minutes.
- Remove the cheesecake from the oven and let it cool completely on a wire rack. Remove the springform pan. Cover with plastic wrap that has been coated with vegetable cooking spray. Refrigerate for at least 3 hours, or up to 2 days.
- To serve, decorate with chocolate curls or candied coffee beans.

Serves 16   5.5 grams of fat per serving

Becky's Summer Peach Trifle

*When this was served at a luncheon at Becky's Hick's, **everyone** wanted the recipe. You can substitute fresh berries for the peaches and have a berry trifle that is equally good. It is best if made a day or two ahead.*

1 **3-ounce box vanilla pudding, made with 1 3/4 cups skim milk**
1 **16-ounce Free & Light Sara Lee Pound Cake**
1/2 **cup orange juice**
8-10 **ripe peaches**
2 **tablespoons lemon juice**

3 **tablespoons honey**
1/2 **cup apricot jam**
1/2 **teaspoon almond flavoring**
1 **12-ounce tub non-dairy whipped topping**
5 **sprigs fresh mint**

- Cook the vanilla pudding and set aside to cool.
- Cut the pound cake into 1-inch slices. Place half of the slices in the bottom of a deep 8-inch glass bowl or trifle dish.
- Pour half of the orange juice over the cake in the bowl.
- Peel and slice the peaches and sprinkle with lemon juice. Reserve a few slices for garnish.
- Microwave the honey and jam for 40 seconds to liquefy. Add the almond flavoring and combine with the peaches.
- Layer half of the peach mixture over the cake in the bowl.
- Mix the cooled vanilla pudding with half of the whipped topping and spread half of the mixture over the top of the peaches in the bowl.
- Repeat the layering process, finishing with the reserved whipped topping. Garnish with the reserved peach slices and and sprigs of fresh mint.

Serves 10   6 grams of fat per serving

Chocolate-Banana Bread Pudding

Early Texas housewives used day-old bread to make bread pudding and it became a favorite dessert of many families. This updated version is delicious, quick and easy to make and has very little fat per serving.

8 slices firm white bread	2 egg whites
Vegetable cooking spray	$^1/_4$ teaspoon salt
4 tablespoons cocoa	1 cup skim milk
4 tablespoons sugar	1 teaspoon vanilla
3 ripe bananas, mashed	Frozen non-fat vanilla yogurt
4 tablespoons non-fat dry milk	

- Cut the bread into 1-inch cubes. Toast for about 15 minutes, or until lightly browned.
- Spray a 9x9-inch baking dish with cooking spray. Spread the bread cubes evenly on the bottom of the dish. Set aside.
- Combine the cocoa, sugar, bananas, non-fat dry milk, egg whites, salt, skim milk and vanilla in a blender or food processor and blend until smooth. Pour over the toasted bread cubes, making sure all sides are coated.
- Bake at 325° for 25 minutes, or until firm.
- Remove from heat and allow to cool slightly. Top with non-fat frozen yogurt and serve while still warm.

Serves 8   1 gram of fat per serving

Floydada Pumpkin Cake Roll

Anne Carthel, who has been Floydada Punkin Day chairwoman for the past two years, contributes this favorite recipe which has been changed slightly to fit the type of low-fat cooking she likes to do for her family. It gives you another good pumpkin dessert.

1 egg	2 teaspoons cinnamon
1/2 cup egg substitute	1 teaspoon ginger
3/4 cup sugar	1/2 teaspoon nutmeg
2/3 cup canned pumpkin	1/2 teaspoon salt
1 teaspoon lemon juice	Vegetable cooking spray
3/4 cup flour	1/2 cup chopped pecans or walnuts
1 teaspoon baking powder	

- Beat the egg and egg substitute at high speed with an electric mixer for 5 minutes. Gradually beat in the sugar, pumpkin and lemon juice.
- Sift together the flour, baking powder, cinnamon, ginger, nutmeg and salt. Add to the the pumpkin mixture and stir until well blended.
- Spread the batter in a 10x15-inch jelly roll pan that has been lined with wax paper or parchment paper, coated with cooking spray and dusted lightly with flour.
- Sprinkle with nuts; bake in a preheated 375° oven for 15 minutes. Turn out immediately onto a towel sprinkled with powdered sugar. Starting at the narrow end, roll the towel and the cake together and cool.

Filling:

2 3-ounce packages Neufchatel (low-fat) cream cheese, softened	3/4 cup powdered sugar
2 tablespoons soft margarine	1/2 teaspoon vanilla

- Beat the cream cheese and margarine together in a small bowl, Add the powdered sugar and vanilla and beat until smooth.
- Unroll the cake. Spread the inside of the roll with the filling. Reroll the cake and sprinkle lightly with more powdered sugar. Cover and chill thoroughly.

Serves 8   12 1/2 grams of fat per serving

Sweets and Treats

During early fall the fields surrounding Floydada are covered with over a million bright orange pumpkins ranging from miniatures of about 1-inch in diameter to giants weighing well over a hundred pounds. After the harvest the town celebrates by throwing a big Punkin Day Party. Pumpkins have been growing in the area for a long time because history records that early Texas President Mirabeau Lamar was leading an expeditionary force across the plains near Floydada when he found Indians feasting on pumpkins they had grown there.

Pumpkin Chiffon Pie

1   envelope unflavored gelatin
$^1/_2$ cup 1% milk
$^2/_3$ cup light brown sugar,
    firmly packed
$^1/_2$ teaspoon salt
$^1/_2$ teaspoon ground cinnamon
$^1/_2$ teaspoon nutmeg
$^1/_2$ teaspoon ginger

$1^1/_2$ cups canned pumpkin
$^1/_3$ cup egg substitute or 3 egg yolks
3   egg whites
$^1/_2$ cup granulated sugar
$^1/_4$ teaspoon maple flavoring
1   8-inch graham cracker pie shell
ReddiWip Lite topping

- Soften the gelatin in a small amount of the milk; add the remainder of the milk and place in a large saucepan.
- Combine the brown sugar, seasonings, pumpkin and egg substitute or egg yolks. Add to the milk and mix thoroughly.
- Cook over medium-high heat, stirring until the mixture boils. Remove from the heat and set aside to cool.
- Beat the egg whites until soft peaks form. Add the sugar gradually and beat until stiff. Add the maple flavoring and beat briefly until blended.
- Fold the meringue mixture into the cooled pumpkin mixture and pour into a prepared graham cracker pie shell.
- Chill for at least 3 hours. Serve with ReddiWip Lite topping.

Serves 8   6 grams of fat with egg substitute - 8 grams of fat with egg yolks

Grapefruit Pie

I was curious when I first heard about grapefruit pie and wondered what it would taste like. With our marvelous grapefruit from the Rio Grande Valley, I decided it would be interesting to try; and I loved it. This unusual dessert is pretty and has a tart, refreshing flavor. The only fat is in the crust; so if you want to trim the fat content, just leave those last few bites of crust uneaten.

1 9-inch pie crust	2 tablespoons cornstarch
3 large pink grapefruit	3 tablespoons strawberry
³/₄ - 1 cup sugar (a little less if	gelatin
grapefruit is sweet)	Non-dairy whipped topping
1 cup water	

- Prepare the pie crust and bake until golden brown.
- Use a sharp knife to peel the grapefruit, removing all the white pith. Cut out each section so it is free of any membrane.
- Drain the grapefruit on paper towels and pat dry. Place the grapefruit sections in the baked pie crust.
- Cook the sugar, water and cornstarch over medium heat until mixture thickens.
- Remove from heat, add the gelatin and stir until dissolved.
- Cool slightly, pour over the grapefruit and chill. Decorate with the topping.

Serves 7   8 grams of fat per serving

A 600-foot cliff in the Palo Duro Canyon provides the backdrop for the spectacular musical drama TEXAS, performed every summer from June through August. A combination of history and pure entertainment portrays the struggles and victories of the early settlers, the cowboys and the Indians. From the time the play opens with a mounted rider with a Texas flag held high galloping across the cliff to meet another rider carrying the United States flag, to the roaring and flashing storm so real members of the audience reach for their raincoats, TEXAS is an exciting extravaganza. For most people, seeing it once is not enough.

Canyon Lemon Chess Pie

My sister, Ada Crager of Canyon sends along this recipe for chess pie that is so smooth and rich you'd think it had twice the grams of fat It does.

1¹/₄ cups sugar	Pinch of salt
1 tablespoon flour	¹/₃ cup lemon juice
1 tablespoon cornmeal	Grated rind of 1 lemon
2 eggs	¹/₄ cup low-fat milk
¹/₂ cup egg substitute	1 Keebler Butter Flavored
4 tablespoons melted margarine	Ready-Crust Pie Shell

- Preheat the oven to 325⁰.
- Combine the sugar, flour and cornmeal in a medium-sized bowl. Whisk the eggs and the egg substitute together until thoroughly mixed.
- Add the margarine, salt, lemon juice and lemon rind to the egg mixture. Combine with the dry ingredients and mix well.
- Stir in the milk until smooth. Pour into the pie shell and bake for 40 to 45 minutes, or until pie is set in the center.

Serves 6   13¹/₂ grams of fat per serving

Sweets and Treats

Most people raised in Texas are gentle and polite and have been taught to "mind your manners" from infancy. Manners in Texas are more a matter of courtesy and respect than rules of etiquette. Children are taught to say "Yes, Ma'am" or "Yes, Sir" to an adult from the time they can talk. On a two-lane highway another Texan will respect your right to be in a hurry and will move over to the shoulder to let you pass easily. You must not forget to give a little wave to say "Thank you." And most important, don't ever ask someone it they are from Texas. If they are, they'll tell you, and if they're not, you don't want to embarass them.

Date Dreams

These cookies are from an old recipe that required no changing to fit our low-fat criteria. They are unusual and always bring comments and compliments.

1 pound dates (about 3 cups), finely chopped	**$^1/_4$ teaspoon salt**
$^3/_4$ cup sugar	**1 cup chopped pecans, toasted**
$^1/_2$ cup flour	**3 egg whites**
$^1/_2$ teaspoon baking powder	**$^1/_2$ teaspoon vanilla**

- Combine the dates, dry ingredients and pecans in a large bowl.
- Beat the egg whites until stiff; add the vanilla and mix. Fold the egg whites into the date mixture until blended.
- Drop by teaspoonful onto a greased cookie sheet, allowing enough room for them to double in size.
- Bake at 325° for 15 minutes.

Makes 5 dozen cookies   1.5 grams of fat per cookie

Date-Nut Bars

These moist, flavorful little bars are great to bake for a picnic because they are easy to transport and they keep well. They are a favorite of anyone who likes dates.

$1/4$ **cup margarine**	$1/2$ **cup flour**
1 **cup brown sugar**	$1/4$ **teaspoon salt**
$1/2$ **cup egg substitute**	1 **teaspoon baking powder**
6 **ounces dates, chopped**	$1/2$ **teaspoon vanilla**
$1/4$ **cup pecans, chopped**	$1/2$ **cup powdered sugar**

- Melt the margarine in a small saucepan. Add the brown sugar and stir over medium heat until smooth. Let mixture cool slightly.
- Stir in the egg substitute, dates and pecans.
- Combine the flour, salt and baking powder; add to the sugar mixture. Stir in the vanilla.
- Spread the date mixture in an 8x8-inch baking pan that has been lightly coated with cooking spray.
- Bake at 350° for 30 to 35 minutes.
- Cool in the pan. Cut into 24 bars. Sieve the powdered sugar onto a plate and roll each bar in it to coat. Tap gently to remove any excess so bars are lightly dusted.

Makes 24 bars   3 grams of fat per bar

Frozen Strawberry Dessert

We have wonderful fresh strawberries most of the time in Texas, but sometimes they are expensive. This recipe uses frozen strawberries, which taste almost as good as the fresh. The pecans and strawberries are a good combination of flavors.

Crust:

1 cup flour	**$^1/_2$ cup margarine**
$^1/_4$ cup brown sugar	**$^1/_2$ cup chopped pecans**

- Mix the crust ingredients thoroughly and press evenly in the bottom of a 9x13-inch baking dish.
- Bake at 350° for 15 minutes. Check after 12 minutes to make sure the crust is browning evenly.
- Allow crust to cool; stir to crumble crust. Reserve $^1/_2$ cup of crumbs for topping. Sprinkle the remaining crumbs in the bottom of the baking dish.

Filling:

2 egg whites	**2$^1/_2$ cups frozen strawberries with juice, thawed**
$^1/_2$ cup sugar	**1$^1/_2$ cups non-dairy whipped topping**
1 teaspoon lemon juice	

- Beat the egg whites until frothy and add the sugar. Continue beating for about 5 minutes, or until stiff.
- Add the lemon juice and thawed strawberries; beat until thick and creamy.
- Fold in the non-dairy topping.
- Spread the filling over the crust crumbs. Sprinkle the reserved crumbs over the top of the filling.
- Freeze for at least 3 hours, or until firm.

Serves 12   11.5 grams of fat per serving

Coffee Tortoni

This is a good dessert to serve when you want a light and luscious dessert that is not filling.

6   egg whites
3   tablespoons instant coffee crystals
$^1/_4$ teaspoon salt
$^1/_2$ cup sugar
2   tablespoons Kahlúa or
      coffee liqueur

$^1/_2$ teaspoon vanilla extract
$^1/_2$ teaspoon almond extract
1   cup Cool Whip or other
      whipped topping
$^1/_4$ cup sliced almonds, toasted
      (reserve 2 tablespoons)

- Combine the egg whites, coffee crystals and salt in a large bowl. Beat with an electric mixer until stiff.
- Graduallly add the sugar while continuing to beat. Add Kahlua or coffee liqueur and almond extract; beat until stiff peaks form.
- Gently fold in the whipped topping and almonds, reserving 2 tablespoons of the almonds for garnish.
- Spoon the mixture in parfait or sherbet glasses, top with the reserved almonds and freeze for 2 to 3 hours.
- Remove from the freezer 20 minutes before serving.

Serves 4
$8^1/_4$ grams of fat per serving

Peppermint Ice Cream

This recipe is so simple I could hardly believe the ice cream is so good. Margaret Kelley of El Paso has made this treat for her family for years, and they love it. It was a hot summer's day when we tested it and all who sampled the result proclaimed it a winner. Mrs. Kelley makes it with whipping cream instead of half & half cream but that adds another 3 grams of fat per serving.

**2 7¹/₂-ounce packages Brach's pepper-
mint Starlight mints or 16-20 ounces
peppermint candy canes**

**¹/₂ gallon homogenized milk
1 pint half & half cream**

- Find someone to help you unwrap all those mints or candy canes. Place them in a large bowl and add the milk. Refrigerate the mixture for 2 to 3 hours, stirring occasionally.
- When the mints or candy canes have dissolved, add the half & half cream.
- Pour the mixture into the freezer container of a 2-quart electric or hand-turned ice cream freezer.
- Freeze according to the manufacturer's instructions. When the paddle stops turning, remove the paddle and pack the freezer with additional ice and rock salt. Let stand for at least 1 hour before serving.

Serves 12
10 grams of fat per serving

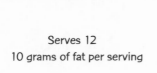

Microwave Pecan Brittle

I had never made candy in a microwave oven until Shirley Clements from out El Paso way called to give me this easy and almost-foolproof recipe. She said it was so good she had just made three batches to share with friends and neighbors. The pecans, with 74 grams of fat per cup, keep it from being low-fat, but they are essential to the recipe. I recommend you make it, then limit the amount you eat.

1 **cup white sugar**	2 **tablespoons margarine**
¹/₂ **cup light corn syrup**	1 **teaspoon vanilla**
1³/₄ **cups chopped pecans**	1 **heaping teaspoon soda**

- Combine the sugar and the syrup in a 2-quart microwave-safe bowl. Mix well.
- Microwave on High for 4 minutes. Remove from the microwave. Add the nuts and mix thoroughly. (Do not be concerned if the mixture seems stiff.)
- Microwave on High for another 4 minutes. Remove from microwave. Add the margarine and vanilla and mix.
- Microwave on High for another 2 minutes. Add the soda and stir. Quickly pour onto a large cookie sheet, spreading as thinly as possible with a spatula and a large spoon.
- Let cool. Break into pieces.

Makes 24 pieces
6.5 grams of fat per piece

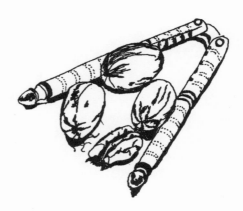

Specialties
of the House

Branding Time

The world's largest collection of rare, original art by Sister M. I. Hummel is located in the Hummel Museum in New Braunfels. Sister Hummel, the German nun whose sketches of children inspired the famous Hummel porcelains, died almost fifty years ago; but the delightful figurines continue to gain in popularity and value. Sieglinde Schöen Smith, who now lives in New Braunfels, was one of the children who inspired Sister Hummel's sketches of children. The owners of the collection, the Nauer family of Switzerland, chose New Braunfels for the museum site because of the efforts of Sieglinde and the commitment of the people of this picturesque German community located in the Texas Hill Country.

Orchard Pear Relish

Marion King, one of the volunteers at the Hummel Museum, contributed this recipe that came from her German mother. It calls for the hard pears usually grown in home orchards. She suggests that the relish be used over cooked beans, black-eyed peas, in a tuna fish salad or on crackers for an appetizer.

16	medium-sized hard pears	$3^1/2$	cups sugar
8	medium red bell peppers	2	teaspoons mustard seed
6	jalapeño or hot green peppers	1	tablespoon salt
6	medium white onions	2	tablespoons cornstarch
4	cups white vinegar		

- Peel and core the pears. Remove the seeds and stems from the peppers. (Use care in handling the jalapeños as the seeds are very irritating to hands and eyes.) Peel the onions. Finely chop the pears, peppers and onions.
- Place the pear mixture in a large stainless or enamel saucepan. Add the vinegar, sugar, mustard seed and salt; mix.
- Cook for 20 minutes over medium-low heat, stirring occasionally. Watch carefully so the mixture does not scorch.
- Add the cornstarch and cook for about 2 minutes, or until thickened.
- Place in sterilized jars, cover with hot paraffin and seal.

Makes 4 pints   0 grams of fat

The Rio Grande was once called Posoge ("river of great water") by the Pueblo Indians, and Rio Bravo by the Mexicans. It also was referred to as Rio Turbio because of its muddy appearance as it neared the Gulf of Mexico. Given the name Rio Grande in the early 1600's by the explorer Juan de Oñate it forms the border between Texas and Mexico for nearly a thousand miles. Somesitmes it rushes through deep canyons, but much of the time it is a sluggish stream, sometimes so narrow that it can be waded. It should never be called the Rio Grande River because the word rio means river.

Minted Grapefruit Slush

A cool, refreshing drink that combines the flavor of mint with the tartness of the good grapefruit grown in the Rio Grande Valley.

1^1/$_4$ cups sugar
^{1}/$_4$ cup light corn syrup
1 cup water
1 teaspoon chopped mint leaves

6 cups fresh grapefruit juice
1 tablespoon grated grapefruit zest
Fresh mint sprigs

- Combine the sugar, corn syrup, water and mint leaves in a large saucepan. Bring to a boil. Remove from heat and let stand for 10 minutes.
- Strain to remove the chopped mint leaves. Add the grapefruit juice and zest; return to the pan and simmer for 10 minutes.
- Pour the mixture into a shallow pan and freeze. When ready to serve, beat with an electric mixer or in a food processor until smooth but still slushy.
- Pour into a large glass. Garnish with the fresh mint sprigs and serve.

Serves 6   0 grams of fat per serving

Texas weather can be an exercise in extremes. West Texas is dry while East Texas can be very wet. It can be so cold in the Panhandle that people vow there is nothing between Amarillo and the North Pole except a barbed wire fence; and in the summer the Big Bend country shows up on national weathercasts as the hottest place in the U.S. However, the good days far outnumber the ones we'd just as soon forget. When Texans were asked to list the ten things they liked best about Texas and the ten things they liked least, weather headed both lists.

Real Freshly Squeezed Lemonade

With so many lemon concentrates, frozen lemonades and lemon-flavored dry mixes available today, a glass of freshly squeezed lemonade from real lemons is a special treat on a hot summer day. This recipe adds zest from lemons and a little mint for a burst of cool, refreshing flavor.

Zest from 2 lemons
1 **cup water**
1 **cup sugar**
1 **cup freshly squeezed lemon juice**

Fresh mint
3 **cups cold water**
Thin slices of lemon

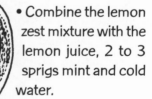

- Carefully strip the thin outer layer of the lemon peel, or zest, from the lemon, using a vegetable peeler or a lemon zester.
- Combine the lemon zest, water and sugar in a small saucepan and bring to a boil. Lower the heat and simmer for 3 to 4 minutes. Cool.

- Combine the lemon zest mixture with the lemon juice, 2 to 3 sprigs mint and cold water.
- Pour into tall, ice-filled glasses and add a sprig of mint and thin slices of lemon.

Serves 6
0 grams of fat per serving

Specialties of the House

Texans love Dr. Pepper. It is marketed all over the country, but the greatest demand is in the South and particularly in Texas. In 1885 a Waco pharmacist who enjoyed experimenting with medicines and beverages concocted a drink called a Waco, and it soon was a favorite of the patrons of Dr. Morrison's drugstore. Dr. Morrison, with several other backers, decided to bottle the new drink and it became a great success. Today, a trip to the Dr. Pepper Museum in Waco is a journey into the past. Artifacts from the original bottling plant, old signs suggesting you drink Dr. Pepper at 10, 2 and 4 , vintage delivery trucks and a real old-fashioned drugstore soda fountain tell a wonderful story of life as it was fifty or sixty years ago. Be sure to take time for a Dr. Pepper float served by a real soda jerk.

Dr. Pepper Soda Fountain Punch

This recipe comes from the COOKING WITH DR. PEPPER AND 7UP cookbook, which naturally features recipes that use the two products as ingredients.

1 quart vanilla ice cream	$1/2$ teaspoon rum extract
7 cups cold Dr. Pepper	

- Place the ice cream in a 4-quart punch bowl. When softened, beat with a rotary beater until smooth.
- Gradually add 2 cups of cold Dr. Pepper, beating until well mixed. Pour in remaining Dr. Pepper and mix well with a spoon.

Serves 20   5 grams of fat per serving

Gail's Sundown Margaritas

Once in a while the sunset in Austin is followed by a flash of lavender in the western sky, giving the city its nickname, "The City of the Violet Crown." If you are lucky enough to enjoy the spectacular scene with one of Gail's Sundown Margaritas in hand, you'll always remember both.

6 **ounces fresh lemon**
   or lime juice
6 **ounces tequila**
4^1/2 **ounces triple sec**

8 **ice cubes**
Salt if desired

- Combine the juice, tequila, triple sec and ice cubes in a tall shaker. Shake vigorously until margaritas are of desired consistency.
- Rub the rims of four glasses with the lime wedges. Place the salt in a saucer. Invert the glasses and turn to coat the rims with salt.
- Fill the glasses with the margaritas, add a lime wedge to each glass and enjoy while watching the sun go down.

Makes 4 regular or 2 Texas-size margaritas   0 grams of fat per serving

Pico de Gallo

For a spicy accompaniment to tacos, fajitas, burritos or practically any Tex-Mex dish, try a little "beak of the cock," the English translation of the name for this Mexican relish. This is a standard but can be tailored to fit your tastebuds by adding fewer or more chilies depending on how fiery you like your salsas. When using fresh chilies, handle them carefully because they can be irritating to your skin and eyes.

3   medium tomatoes, peeled and chopped
3   green onions, chopped
3   garlic cloves, minced

2   tablespoons chopped fresh cilantro
1   tablespoon lime juice
1 or 2 jalapeños, seeded and chopped

• Combine all the ingredients in a medium-sized bowl. Chill for several hours before serving. Pico de Gallo will keep for at least 2 weeks if refrigerated.

Makes 3 cups   0 grams of fat per serving

Salsa Verde

It will come as no surprise to Texans that last year more salsas were sold in the United States than catsups. We eat a lot of ready-made salsa with our tortilla chips, hamburgers, huevos rancheros and Tex-Mex favorites; but once in a while we want one that's a little different, like this one with tomatillos.

2   teaspoons salad oil
1   medium onion, minced
1   garlic clove, minced
1   cup canned tomatillos, diced

1   4-ounce can chopped green chilies
1   tablespoon fresh cilantro, chopped
Salt and pepper to taste

• Combine all the ingredients and chill for several hours before serving.

Makes 1¹/2 cups   ¹/2 gram of fat per serving

Shrimp Cocktail Sauce

This easy and tasty sauce can be put together in just minutes and it is good with almost any seafood.

1 **cup catsup**	1 **tablespoon lemon juice**
1 **tablespoon prepared horseradish**	1 **teaspoon Worcestershire sauce**
	2 or 3 drops Tabasco sauce

- Combine all the ingredients in a small bowl and mix until blended.
- Refrigerate until ready to serve.

Makes 1 1/4 cups   Fat free

Horseradish Sauce

1/2 **cup Hellmann's Reduced Fat Mayonnaise**	1/2 **teaspoon dry mustard**
1/2 **cup light sour cream**	1 **teaspoon lemon juice**
	3 **tablespoons prepared horseradish**

- Combine all the ingredients in a small bowl. Refrigerate until ready to serve.

Makes about 1 cup   2 1/2 grams of fat per serving

San Antonio, with its mixture of Mexican and European flavors, its wonderful old missions and the Alamo, is the favorite Texas city of most visitors. The popular River Walk winding its way through the heart of the city is lined with sidewalk restaurants, hotels and shops. Flat-bottomed chalupa boats, some carrying food and drink and colorful mariachi musicians, drift under the arched bridges and allow their passergers to see San Antonio the easy way. During the Christmas season luminarios outline the Walk and bridges, and hundreds of thousands of tiny lights twinkle from the trees along the riverbanks, turning the scene into one of enchantment. San Antonio is a city that loves fiestas and just any excuse will do. No wonder it is considered one of the most unique cities in the country.

Tomatillo Sauce

Tomatillos are small, firm yellow or green tomatoes wrapped in papery husks with a tart, fresh flavor similar to limes. They have long been used in Mexican cooking, but good cooks everywhere are discovering their sharp, unique taste adds zing to a number of dishes.

12-16 fresh tomatillos
1   large onion, chopped
1   4.5-ounce can chopped green chilies

2 garlic cloves, minced
1 tablespoon chopped cilantro
$^1/_2$ cup chicken broth
Salt and pepper to taste

- Remove the husks from the tomatillos. Drop them in boiling water for 1 minute. Cut into quarters.
- Purée the tomatillos, onion, garlic, green chilies, cilantro and 2 tablespoons of the chicken broth in a food processor until smooth.
- Pour the mixture into a small saucepan. Add the remaining chicken broth and simmer for 10 minutes. Add salt and pepper to taste. Serve as a sauce or as a condiment on meats, fish, or any Mexican food.

Makes 2 cups   0 grams of fat per serving

Mango Chutney

It's so easy to make chutney in the microwave you'll probably never use the stove-top method again. The flavor of the mangoes in this sweet-spicy chutney is a good acompaniment to poultry or pork dishes.

1 1/2 **cups chopped fresh mangoes**	2 **tablespoons white vinegar**
1/4 **cup light brown sugar**	1/2 **teaspoon ground ginger**
1/4 **cup finely chopped onion**	1/2 **teaspoon dry mustard**
1/2 **cup golden raisins**	

- Peel and seed the mangoes and cut into 1/2-inch cubes. Combine with the other ingredients in a deep 2-quart microwave-safe dish. Mix well.
- Cook, uncovered, on High for 6 minutes. Cool, cover and refrigerate.

Makes about 2 cups   0 grams of fat per serving

Pickled Beets

2 16-ounce cans sliced beets
1 cup cider vinegar
³/₄ cup brown sugar

1 teaspoon whole allspice
10 whole cloves
1 cinnamon stick, 2 inches long

- Drain the beets, reserving the juice.
- Combine the beet juice with the remaining ingredients in a medium-sized saucepan. Bring to a boil over medium heat.
- Spoon the beets into 2 clean pint jars and pour the juice mixture over them.
- Seal the jars and refrigerate for several days for flavors to blend.

Makes 1 quart   0 grams of fat per serving

Pickled Peaches

1 cup cider vinegar
1 cup water
2 cups sugar
1 teaspoon ground cloves

1 quart peaches, peeled
6 whole cloves
2 cinnamon sticks

- Combine the vinegar, water, sugar and ground cloves in a stainless steel or enamel pan and boil for 10 minutes.
- Add the peaches to the syrup and cook for 20 to 25 minutes, or until tender.
- Pack the peaches in 2 sterilized pint jars. Add 3 whole cloves and a cinnamon stick to each jar. Cover the peaches with syrup.
- Seal immediately. Allow 2 weeks or more before serving.

Makes 2 pints   0 grams of fat per serving

Faye's Pickled Okra

Faye Robertson of Temple learned the art of canning when she was a young girl helping her mother on their farm, and she makes these wonderful crisp pickles from small, tender okra pods. She leaves a little of the stem on the pod for easier handling.

1^1/2 **pounds fresh young okra**	1 **quart white vinegar**
6 **garlic cloves**	1 **cup water**
6 **small red or green hot peppers**	^{1}/2 **cup salt**
6 **teaspoons dill seed**	

- Prepare the okra by washing with a brush or nylon net to remove the "fuzz." Trim the okra stems, leaving about ^{1}/2-inch attached to the pod.
- Sterilize 6 pint jars.
- Into each jar pack 1 garlic clove, 1 small pepper, 1 teaspoon dill seed and enough okra to fill the jar. Pack the first layer of okra in the jar with the stems down and fill in second layer with the stems up.
- Bring the vinegar, water and salt to a boil in an enamel or stainless steel pan and simmer for 5 minutes. Pour the hot mixture over the okra.
- Immediately seal the jars. Store in a dark place for at least 3 weeks before serving.

Makes 6 pints

0 grams of fat per serving

Stove-Top Apple Butter

12 large Granny Smith apples
1 cup frozen apple juice concentrate
2 tablespoons lemon juice

1 cup brown sugar
1 1/2 teaspoons cinnamon
1/4 teaspoon salt
1/4 teaspoon allspice

- Peel, core and slice the apples into a large, heavy kettle. Add the apple juice concentrate.
- Place the kettle over medium heat and bring the mixture to a boil.
- Reduce the heat and simmer for 20 minutes, or until the apples are tender.
- Place the hot mixture in a food processer or blender and purée briefly. Leave some small chunks to add to the texture. Return the apple mixture to the kettle.
- Stir in the remaining ingredients and cook, stirring often, over low heat for about 30 minutes or until mixture thickens. Watch carefully for the mixture will scorch easily as it begins to thicken.

Makes 7 cups   0 grams of fat per serving

Crimson Raspberry Sauce

An attractive sauce that can be used over fresh peaches, angel food and pound cakes or Melva's Raspberry Bombe (see Index).

**1   10-ounce package frozen
   raspberries, thawed**

1   tablespoon cornstarch
1/2 cup red currant jelly

- Crush the berries with the back of a slotted spoon and place in a medium-sized saucepan. Blend in the cornstarch and the currant jelly.
- Cook and stir over medium heat until the sauce is bubbly. Continue to cook for another minute until the sauce is clear and thickened.
- Remove seeds by straining through a coarse sieve. Cool.

Makes 2 cups   0 grams of fat per serving

Fresh Mint Sauce

The tangy flavor of fresh mint is good with any number of meat dishes. This is more tart than mint jelly.

**1/3 cup finely chopped fresh
   mint leaves**
1/4 cup white vinegar
2   tablespoons sugar

3/4 cup water
1   tablespoon cornstarch
1/4 cup red currant jelly

- Combine the mint leaves, vinegar, sugar and water in a small saucepan. Moisten the cornstarch with a little of the mixture and add, blending well.
- Place over medium heat and cook, stirring frequently, until the sauce is clear and begins to thicken. Add the currant jelly; stir until melted.
- Refrigerate what you don't plan to use immediately.

Makes 1 1/2- 2 cups   0 grams of fat per serving

Yogurt Cheese

Yogurt cheese has the consistency of cream cheese but none of the fat. It can be substituted for cream cheese, sour cream or mayonnaise in many recipes. It's simple to make and keeps for 1 to 2 weeks in the refrigerator. If you want to use it in cooking, add 1 teaspoon of cornstarch for each cup of cheese to prevent separation while cooking.

2 cups non-fat yogurt that does not contain gelatin or stabilizer

- Line a strainer with a coffee filter or cheesecloth. Set the strainer over a deep bowl.
- Spoon the yogurt into the coffee filter; cover with plastic film and refrigerate.
- Allow yogurt to drain for 8 to 10 hours or until the cheese reaches the desired consistency. The longer it drains the thicker it will become.

Makes 1 cup   0 grams of fat

Cream Sauce or Soup Substitute

This recipe gives you a fat-free base for sauces, soups and casseroles. You can vary the taste by adding the seasonings you prefer. It keeps in the refrigerator indefinitely. Just mix it with water and heat when needed.

1 cup instant non-fat dry milk
1 tablespoon dried onion flakes
6 tablespoons cornstarch
1/4 teaspoon black pepper

2 tablelspoons instant chicken bouillon (low-sodium)
1/2 teaspoon basil (optional)
1/2 teaspoon thyme (optional)

- Combine all the ingredients and store in a tightly covered container in the refrigerator.
- To use, mix 1/3 cup of the dry base with 1 1/4 cups water and stir over low heat until thickened.

Makes 1 1/2 cups dry mix   0 grams of fat per serving

Special Vinegars

Special vinegars are a wonderful addition to a pantry shelf. They can be found in gourmet sections of large grocery stores and specialty cooking shops; or they are simple and inexpensive to make yourself. One of the nicest gifts you can offer a friend or hostess is your own special vinegar in an interesting bottle. With a little experimentation, you will discover how much the special flavors add to your favorite recipes.

HERBAL VINEGAR: Tuck several sprigs of freshly picked herbs (tarragon, basil, rosemary or dill) stem first into 4 or 5 small bottles. Partly crush a few of the herbs to add more flavor. Heat 4 cups of cider or white vinegar in a stainless steel pan until it begins to simmer; do not allow it to boil. Pour the heated vinegar over the herbs in the bottles, seal and let cool. Allow the vinegar to stand for several days for full flavor to develop.

Makes 1 quart
0 grams of fat

GARLIC & PEPPER VINEGAR: To add more interest to the Herbal Vinegar, add peeled garlic cloves and fresh, small hot peppers to the herbs before adding the hot vinegar.

BERRY VINEGAR: In a blender, purée 2 cups of raspberries, strawberries or blueberries with 2 cups of white vinegar. Pour into a 2-quart bottle; add another 2 cups of vinegar and cover. Allow to mature for 3 to 4 weeks. Strain into smaller bottles.

Makes 5 cups
0 grams of fat

Chicken Broth

Chicken and beef broth are important in low-fat cooking; and while canned broths and instant bouillon granules may be used, your own broth will taste better and cost less. You'll find that whole chickens are one of the best buys in your meat counter. Remove and reserve the breast meat before placing the remaining chicken in the soup kettle. After the broth is prepared, freeze or use as a base for soups, casseroles and vegetables.

1 **whole chicken or stewing hen**	**Chunks of carrots, onions or vege-**
8 **cups water**	**tables you have been saving**
1 **cup chopped celery leaves, green**	1 **tablespoon lemon juice**
onion tops and parsley	

- Remove giblets from inside the cavity of the chicken. Debone the breast portion for later use. Place remaining chicken and giblets, except liver, in a large soup kettle.
- Add water, vegetable broth and vegetables. Bring to a boil. Reduce the heat and simmer for 1 hour, skimming when necessary.
- Remove the chicken from the broth, cool enough to handle and pull the meat from the bones. Reserve for later use.
- Return the bones to the kettle; continue to simmer until broth is reduced by about one-third.
- Strain broth into a large bowl; refrigerate.
- Remove fat that rises to the top and solidifies, leaving you fat-free, sodium-free broth to use as needed. Freeze any broth you will not use within 3 to 4 days.

Makes 5 cups   0 grams of fat per serving

Index

Index

Muffins —
  Bran, Plano, 24
  Oatmeal, Salado, 25
Mushrooms —
  New Potatoes with Mushrooms, 103
  Mushroom-Stuffed Shells, 12
  Spinach-Stuffed Mushrooms, 13
Mustang Island Black Bean Relish, 116
Mustard Dill Sauce, 60
          — N —
Nancy Jo's Chicken Salad, 70
Nectarine Sauce, 31
New Potatoes with Mushrooms, 103
Nick's Seasoned Oyster Crackers, 15
Not-to-Worry Fried Potatoes, 106
          — O —
Oatmeal Muffins, Salado, 25
Okra, Black-Eyed Peas with, 112
Okra, Faye's Pickled, 157
Old El Paso Dip, 4
Onions, Creamy Baked, 117
Orchard Pear Relish, 147
          — P —
Pancakes, Three-Grain, 30
Panchos, 14
Pan-Grilled Chicken Breasts, 68
Panhandle Carrot Cake, 126

Parfait, Pecos Cantaloupe-Strawberry, 127
Paris Cornbread with Green Chilies, 22
Pasta —
  Broccoli-Tomato Sauce, Pasta with, 94
  Chicken Pasta Salad, 71
  Marv's Seafood, 59
Pavlova, Lake Travis, 121
Peach-Blueberry Crisp, 129
Peaches, Pickled, 156
Peach Trifle, Becky's, 132
Pear Relish, Orchard, 147
Pecan Brittle, Microwave, 143
Pecos Cantaloupe-Strawberry Parfait, 127
Pepper Medley, 111
Peppered Fish with Creamy Dill Sauce, 60
Peppermint Ice Cream, 142
Phyl's Glazed Lemon Bundt Cake, 124
Pickled Beets, 156
Pickled Okra, Faye's, 157
Pickled Peaches, 156
Pico de Gallo, 152
Pies —
  Canyon Lemon Chess Pie, 137
  Grapefruit Pie, 136
  Pumpkin Chiffon Pie, 135
Pita Crisps, 17
Pita Pockets, Tuna-Tomato, 91

Index of Tales

So many people have helped and encouraged me in the writing of this book and I am blessed to have their support. I want to especially thank Mary Ullrich for her fine editing; for punctuating, polishing and proofing. This is the fourth book she has edited for me, and her patience and professionalism are very special. It would have been impossible to typeset the book without Pete Lewis, Sally Sykes and Debbie Stevens coming to my rescue while I was learning PageMaker, a new computer program. Then there were friends like Bev Dorsey, who not only helped me find several recipes but tested and proofed them with me. I am grateful to those mentioned and many others who were there when I needed them.

Acknowledgments

With special thanks to the following for recipes from their cookbooks or restaurants:

Jean Durkee for the Vegetable Medley recipe from her cookbook ***Tout dé Suite a la Microwave***

Cynthia Pedregon for allowing me to convert the Jalapeño-Potato Soup recipe from ***The Peach Tree Tearoom Cookbook***

The Dr. Pepper/Seven-Up Companies for allowing use of their Soda Fountain Punch recipe from ***COOKING WITH DR. PEPPER AND 7UP***

Catherine LeDerer for her Wedding Fajitas recipe from the cookbook ***Symbols of Sharing***

The Pelican's Landing Restaurant of Port Aransas for the Mustang Island Black Bean Relish recipe by Bill Stephens

Frank's Place in La Grange for the Frank's Place Cucumber Salad recipe

And thank you to the following for information for Texas stories:

The Hummel Museum of New Braunfels
The Marine Military Academy Visitor's Center of Harlingen
The West of the Pecos Museum of Pecos

Contributors

My deepest thanks to all the great Texas cooks who shared their favorite recipes with me. Many gave me several so I could have a choice, and I'm sorry we could not use them all. The most interesting part of writing a cookbook is collecting the recipes and getting to know the men and women who sent them to me from all over the state.

Joyce Andrews	Houston	Kelley Jemison	Westlake Hills
Margie Barnes	Lakeway	Mrs. Lyndon B. Johnson	Stonewall
Nancy Jo Barrington	Houston	Margaret Kelley	El Paso
J. Robert Buckley	Brownsville	Margie Kelley	El Paso
Dennis Burdette	Carrollton	Sue Carole Kidd	Amarillo
Kandy Burdette	Carrollton	Marion King	Cibolo
Anne Carthel	Floydada	Bobbie Lair	Lakeway
Billie Christopher	Marfa	Catherine LeDerer	Paris
Ada Crager	Canyon	Gene Long	Houston
Karen Crager	Houston	Helen Mann	Paris
Dale Culwell	Houston	Lemma Nite	San Marcos
Georgia Denton	LaGrange	Cynthia Pedregon	Fredericksburg
Bev Dorsey	Lakeway	Genora Previt	Pecos
Jean Durkee	Austin	Kay Rester	Lakeway
Nancy Elcan	Lakeway	Melva Ribe	Lakeway
Suzi Epps	Salado	Mary Lou Rivera	San Antonio
Dot Fields	Lakeway	Faye Robertson	Temple
Kay Germond	Lakeway	Ann Rowland	Lakeway
Jean Griffen	Plano	Nancy Smith	Amarillo
Gerry Groden	Austin	Diane Speer	Conroe
Leona Hand	Harlingen	Linda Taylor	Houston
Dolores Hartley	Marshall	Peg Tolzmann	Lakeway
Marv Hein	Lakeway	Mindy Walls	Fort Worth
Becky Hicks	Lakeway	Joanie Warneke	Waco
Phyllis Hook	Lakeway	Wylene Williams	Salado
Virginia Hughes	Gruene	Sam & Sylvia Wisialowski	Spring

If you would like to order additional copies of **New Tastes of Texas**, we have included an order blank below.

Heinco, Inc.
101 Explorer Cove
Austin, TX. 78734

Please send _____ copies of *New Tastes of Texas to:*

Name_____

Address_____

City_____State_____Zip Code_____

Enclosed is $14.95 plus $2.00 for postage and handling. Texas residents should add an additional $1.12 for sales tax.

If you enjoyed this book by Peg Hein and Kathryn Lewis, you might also like to have these earlier books:

Name of Book	Price	Postage & Handling	Quantity
Tastes & Tales From Texas....With Love	12.00	2.25	_____
MORE Tastes & Tales From Texas	12.00	2.25	_____
Life's Too Short Not To Live It As a Texan	7.00	2.00	_____

Texas residents should add $7^1/2$% sales tax. Please send your order and check to:
Heinco, Inc., 101 Explorer Cove, Austin, TX. 78734.
Thank you.